This student workbook is intended to reinforce your learning of the content in the three units of the single award GCSE Additional Science specification (2103), from Edexcel.

Every worksheet is cross-referenced to the revision and classroom companion, *Edexcel GCSE Additional Science,* published by Letts and Lonsdale.

The worksheets for each unit are divided into four topics to correspond with the specification and revision guide, and provide a clear, manageable structure to your revision. The questions are varied in style to keep your study interesting and there is limited space for each question, so you will have to think carefully about your answers.

At the end of each topic there is an activity, e.g. a crossword, so that you can test your knowledge of the key words and concepts.

> Throughout this workbook, any questions covering content that is limited to the Higher Tier exam papers appear inside a shaded box, clearly labelled with the symbol HT.

At the end of the book, you will find a detailed periodic table which will provide a useful reference as you work through the chemistry worksheets.

This workbook focuses on the material which is externally assessed (i.e. tested under exam conditions). It does not cover the practical skills assessment and assessment activities, which are marked by your teacher.

A Note to Teachers

The pages in this workbook can be used as…

- classwork sheets – students can use the revision guide to answer the questions
- harder classwork sheets – pupils study the topic and then answer the questions without using the revision guide

- easy-to-mark understanding and reinforce their learning
- the basis for learning homework tasks which are then tested in subsequent lessons
- test materials for topics or entire units
- a structured revision programme prior to the objective tests / written exams.

Answers to these worksheets are available to order.

ISBN 978-1-905129-76-8

Published by Letts and Lonsdale.

Authors / Consultants: Dr Ron Holt, Susan Loxley and Aleksander Jedrosz
Project Editor: Rebecca Skinner
Cover and Concept Design: Sarah Duxbury
Design: Little Red Dog Design

© Lonsdale, a division of Huveaux Plc 2006, 2008. All rights reserved. No part of this publication may be reproduced, stored in a retrieval system, or transmitted by any means, electronic, mechanical, photocopying, recording, or otherwise without the prior written permission of Lonsdale.

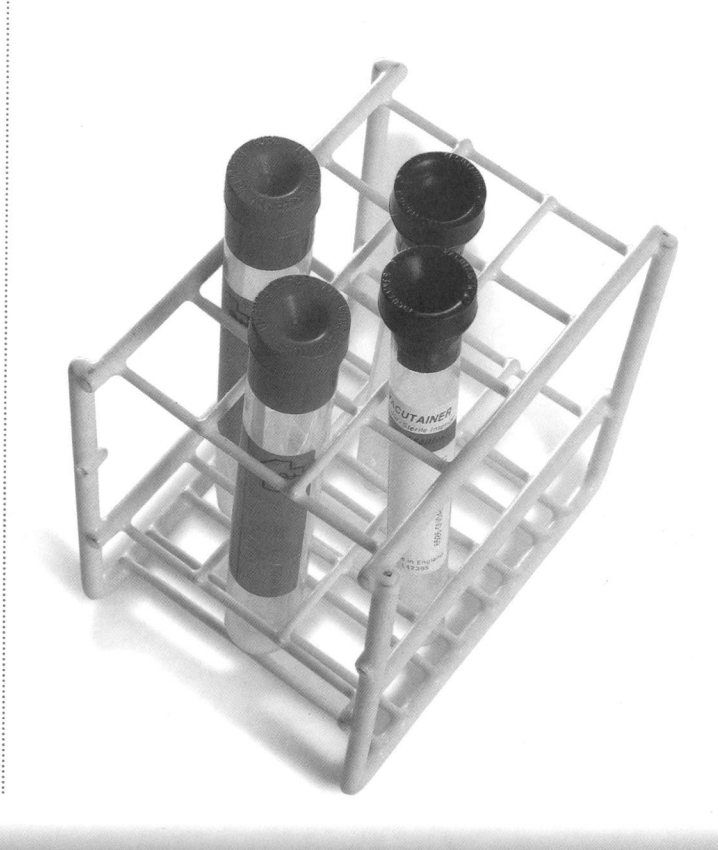

Contents

Contents

Biology

Unit B2
- 4 Topic 1: Inside Living Cells
- 11 Topic 2: Divide and Develop
- 19 Topic 3: Energy Flow
- 26 Topic 4: Interdependence

Chemistry

Unit C2
- 32 Topic 5: Synthesis
- 42 Topic 6: In Your Element
- 51 Topic 7: Chemical Structures
- 56 Topic 8: How Fast? How Furious?

Physics

Unit P2
- 64 Topic 9: As Fast As You Can!
- 75 Topic 10: Roller Coasters and Relativity
- 82 Topic 11: Putting Radiation to Use
- 89 Topic 12: Power of the Atom

- 96 Periodic Table

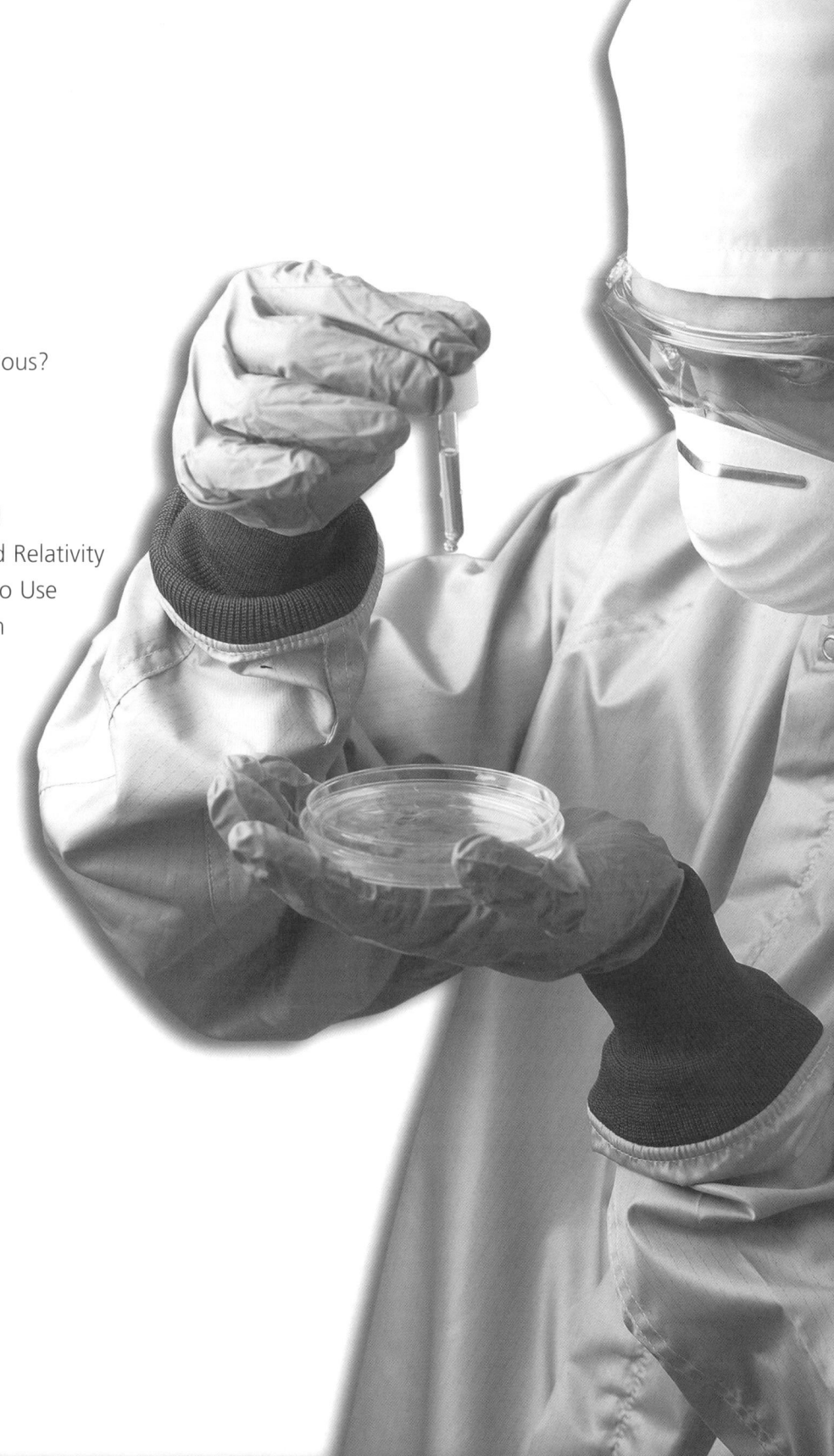

Inside Living Cells

1 a) Explain, as fully as you can, what genes are.

b) What are chromosomes?

c) How many chromosomes would you find in a human skin cell?

2 Fill in the gaps in the passage below, which describes a DNA molecule.

A DNA molecule consists of two which coil around each other to form a

. They are joined together by crosslinks formed from pairs of .

3 Unscramble the letters to find the names of the four bases. Alongside each one, write the name of the base it always pairs with.

a) INNEEDA   Pairs with:

b) NUINAGE   Pairs with:

c) NICETOYS   Pairs with:

d) MINTYEH   Pairs with:

4 The sequence (order) of the base pairs in DNA is different from molecule to molecule. In your own words, explain the significance of the sequence of bases.

5 What does the body need proteins for?

Inside Living Cells

1 a) What is an organelle? _____

b) Which organelles are involved in protein synthesis?

_____

2 Each statement below describes a different stage in the replication of DNA for protein synthesis. Number them **1** to **5** to show the correct sequence of events.

a) The RNA moves out of the nucleus into the cell's cytoplasm. ☐

b) Amino acids are joined together in the correct order to form a specific protein. ☐

c) A section of the DNA molecule 'unzips'. ☐

d) The base code is deciphered by the ribosomes. ☐

e) A copy of the coding strand is made in the form of a molecule of RNA. ☐

3 Give two important differences between DNA and RNA.

a) _____

b) _____

4 Summarise, with the help of diagrams, the three main stages in the mass production of insulin by genetic engineering.

Stage 1: _____

Stage 2: _____

Stage 3: _____

Inside Living Cells

1 a) In your own words, describe what a fermenter is.

b) Complete the table below, to show what features a fermenter has and why. The first one has been done for you.

Feature	Purpose
i) Sterile Air Supply	Provides oxygen for respiration. Ensures aseptic conditions (no contamination).
ii) Nutrient Medium	
iii) Stirrer	
iv) Temperature Probe	
v) pH Probe	
vi) Water-cooled Jacket	
vii) Outlet Tap	

2 In wine and beer making, yeast is used to ferment glucose (from grapes or malted barley) to produce alcohol. Yeast is also used in bread-making. Explain why alcohol is not produced when bread is baked.

3 List three advantages to using microorganisms in food production.

a)

b)

c)

Inside Living Cells

1) This is the word equation for the chemical reaction that takes place during aerobic respiration.

Glucose + Oxygen ⟶ Carbon dioxide + Water

a) Write a symbol equation for this reaction.

b) What else is produced during aerobic respiration, and what is it used for?

c) Explain, in as much detail as you can, where the glucose and oxygen come from and how they get to respiring cells.

d) By what process do the reactants and products of aerobic respiration enter and leave the cells?

e) What does the body do with the waste products of aerobic respiration?

HT

f) Referring back to part d), explain what happens at a cellular level when respiration takes place at an increased rate.

Inside Living Cells

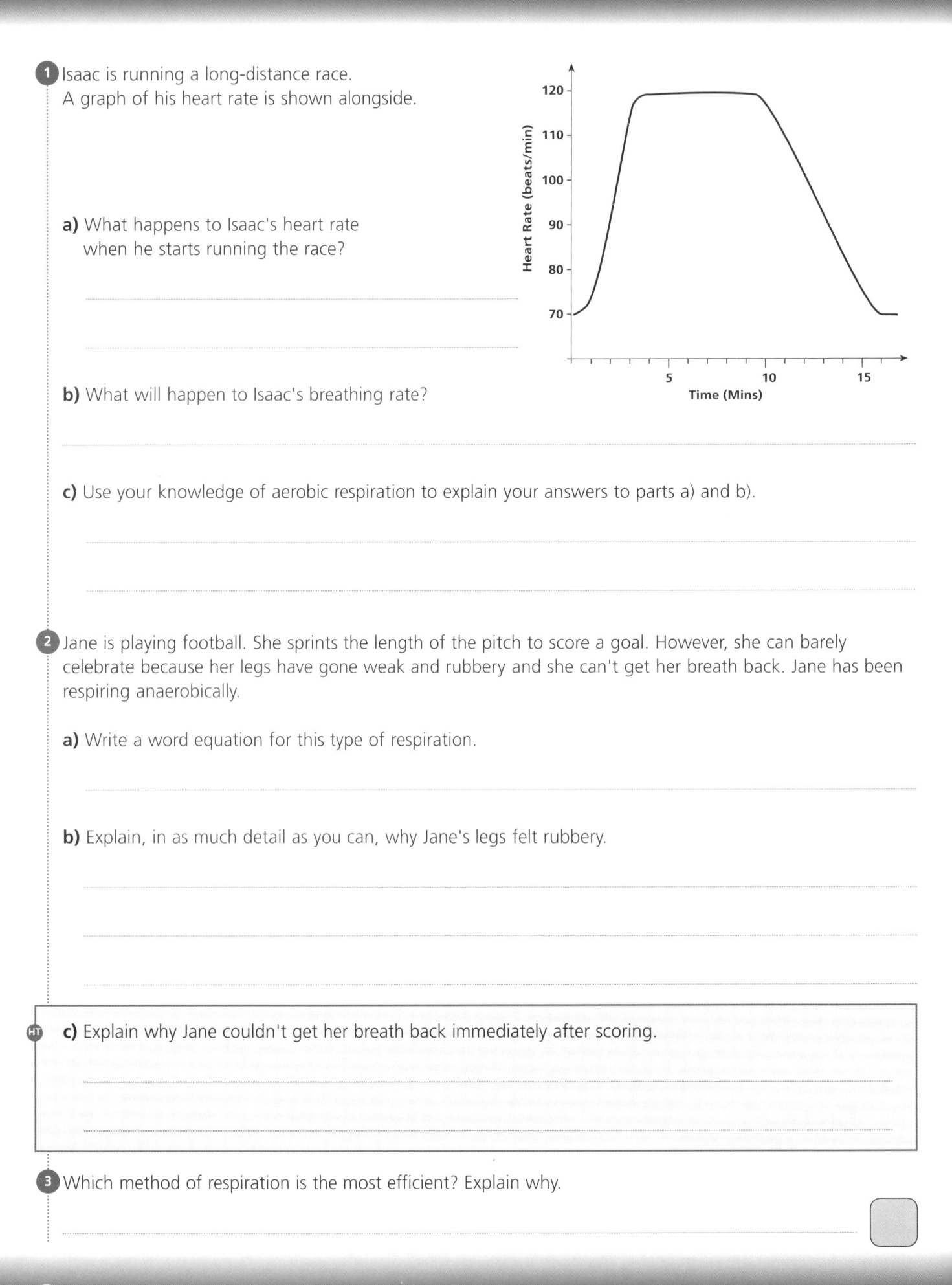

1) Isaac is running a long-distance race.
A graph of his heart rate is shown alongside.

a) What happens to Isaac's heart rate when he starts running the race?

b) What will happen to Isaac's breathing rate?

c) Use your knowledge of aerobic respiration to explain your answers to parts a) and b).

2) Jane is playing football. She sprints the length of the pitch to score a goal. However, she can barely celebrate because her legs have gone weak and rubbery and she can't get her breath back. Jane has been respiring anaerobically.

a) Write a word equation for this type of respiration.

b) Explain, in as much detail as you can, why Jane's legs felt rubbery.

HT c) Explain why Jane couldn't get her breath back immediately after scoring.

3) Which method of respiration is the most efficient? Explain why.

Inside Living Cells

1 After school and at weekends, Simon likes to play games on his computer with his friends. He doesn't like to stop in the middle of a game, so he often skips dinner and eats snacks like crisps and biscuits instead.

Simon's mum takes him for a check up at the health centre. The nurse tells him he is in danger of becoming obese.

a) What is obesity?

b) Think about Simon's lifestyle, and give two factors that are contributing towards him becoming obese.

　　i)

　　ii)

c) The nurse tells Simon that he must ensure he eats a balanced diet. What does this mean?

d) Why is it particularly important for a teenager like Simon to eat a balanced diet?

e) What other advice would you give him to avoid becoming obese and why?

2 Suggest two reasons why official advice about diet and exercise has changed over time.

　　a)

　　b)

Inside Living Cells

1 Complete the crossword below.

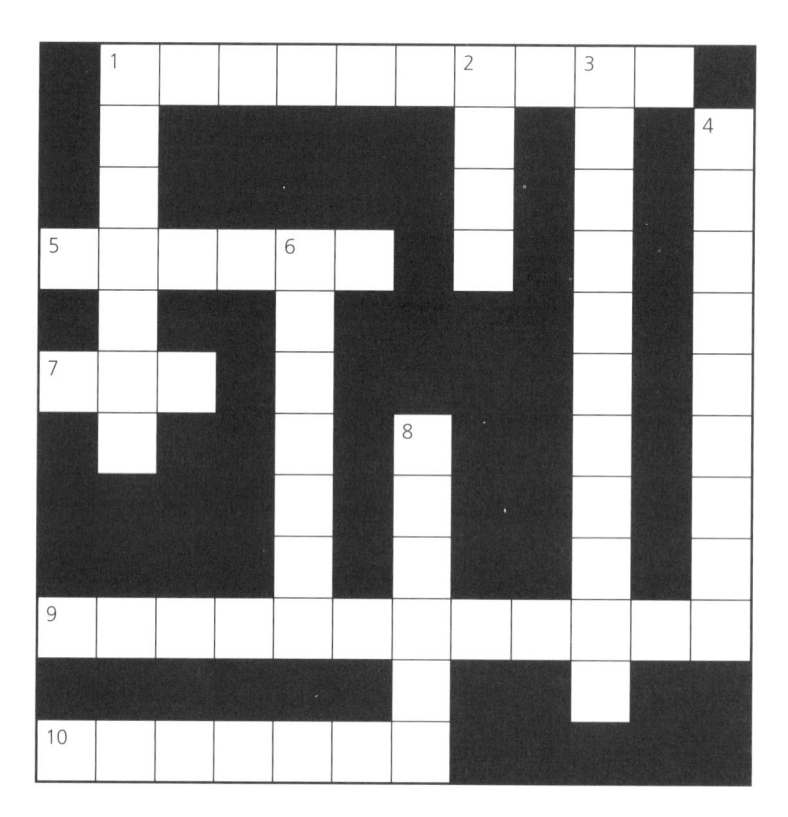

Across
1. Cells join these molecules together to form proteins. (5,5)
5. The purpose of respiration is to produce this. (6)
7. The material that chromosomes (and genes) are made from. (3)
9. The process by which the composition of a medium changes as microorganisms extract some substances and release others through respiration. (12)
10. This type of respiration uses oxygen to convert glucose to energy efficiently. (7)

Down
1. One of the four bases found in DNA; it pairs up with thymine. (7)
2. The sequence of bases in a DNA molecule acts as one of these. (4)
3. Describes the shape of 7 across. (6,5)
4. The process by which the gaseous exchange of oxygen and carbon dioxide takes place in respiring cells. (9)
6. One of the four bases found in DNA; it pairs with cytosine. (7)
8. This type of acid is produced as a result of anaerobic respiration. (6)

Divide and Develop

1 The following statements refer to mitosis. Complete the explanation by drawing a diagram to illustrate each stage.

a) Parent cell with two pairs of chromosomes.	**b)** Each chromosome replicates itself.	**c)** The copies separate and the cell divides.	**d)** Genetically identical daughter cells are formed.

HT

2 Write **mitosis**, **meiosis** or **both** alongside each of the following statements as appropriate.

   a) A type of cell division.

   b) Involved in asexual reproduction.

   c) A diploid cell divides to produce further diploid cells.

   d) Involved in sexual reproduction.

   e) A diploid cell divides to produce haploid cells.

   f) Produces genetically identical clones.

   g) Needed for growth and cell replacement.

3 Why must meiosis occur before fertilisation?

4 Write **true** or **false** alongside each of the following statements, as appropriate.

   a) A normal body cell is an example of a haploid cell.

   b) A gamete is an example of a haploid cell.

   c) A diploid cell contains two sets of chromosomes.

   d) Cells produced by meiosis are genetically identical.

   e) Cells produced by mitosis are genetically different.

Divide and Develop

1 Unscramble the letters below to find three ways in which cells help an organism to grow and develop, and write a brief description of each process.

a) PAINASICETOLIS

....

....

b) NOAXESNIP

....

....

c) ISINVOID

....

....

2 a) Why is length or height not an accurate measure of growth?

....

b) Why is wet mass usually used to measure growth, when dry mass is a more accurate measurement?

....

....

3 Sketch graphs to show what you would expect the rate of growth for **a)** an elephant, and **b)** a redwood tree, to be over its lifetime.

a)

b)

c) Explain the difference (if any) in the shapes of your graphs.

....

....

Divide and Develop

1 a) There are two types of factor that can affect the growth and development of an organism. What are they?

　　i) ....　　ii) ....

b) Write **nature**, **nurture** or **both** alongside each of these characteristics as appropriate.

　　i) Eye colour　..................................　　ii) Height　..................................

　　iii) Colour of skin　..................................　　iv) Shape of earlobes　..................................

　　v) Scars　..................................　　vi) Weight　..................................

2 Bhavna is a new born baby. She is 48cm long. List three factors that will determine how tall she grows to be as an adult.

　　a) ....

　　b) ....

　　c) ....

3 a) A plant's genes determine its potential height. Complete the table below to show what other resources it needs to be able to achieve this height.

Resource	Why the Plant Needs It	How the Plant Obtains It
i)	For photosynthesis	
ii) Carbon dioxide		
iii)	For respiration	
iv)		Root cells absorb these from the soil
v) Temperature (warmth)		

b) Explain how the availability of these resources affects the distribution of plants.

....

....

....

....

Divide and Develop

1) Describe two ways in which synthetic plant hormones can be used to produce large quantities of ripe fruit for supermarkets all year round.

a) _____

b) _____

2) A cyclist in the Tour de France failed a drugs test because it showed abnormally high levels of the male sex hormone testosterone. Although it is banned, some sports people use a synthetic version of the hormone, which can increase muscle growth.

a) Why do you think a cyclist might take a synthetic version of testosterone?

_____

b) Give three other reasons why a professional cyclist might consider taking a banned drug.

i) _____

ii) _____

iii) _____

c) Why do you think there is a greater risk involved if sportswomen take these synthetic hormones compared to sportsmen?

_____

d) Professional sports people can be tested for drugs at any time, not just when they are competing. Why do you think this is?

_____

e) Why is it morally wrong for sports people to take banned drugs?

_____

Divide and Develop

1 a) *Plants have the ability to regenerate.* Explain what this statement means.

....

b) Name three types of animal that have the ability to regenerate body parts.

i) .... ii) .... iii) ....

2 a) What is a stem cell?

....

....

b) Apart from their general structure, how are animal stem cells different to plant stem cells?

....

....

c) Why do scientists think that stem cells could be very useful in the field of medicine?

....

3 Normal human cells can divide about 52 times. This is called the Hayflick limit. As cells approach this limit they begin ageing and eventually lose the ability to divide, and start to die.

a) How does the Hayflick limit apply to cancer cells?

....

b) With reference to your answer for part a), why are cancer cells so dangerous?

....

....

c) How does the Hayflick limit apply to stem cells?

....

d) In terms of using stem cells in medicine, is your answer to part c) an **advantage** or a **disadvantage**? Explain your answer.

....

....

© Lonsdale   ADDITIONAL SCIENCE WORKBOOK - Revision Guide Reference: Page 15

Divide and Develop

1 What is meant by the term 'selective breeding'?

....

....

2 Selective breeding is used in farming to make food production more efficient. For each of the examples below, state whether the aim is to increase **quality**, **quantity** or **yield**.

   a) Selectively breeding cows to produce the richest, creamiest milk possible. ....

   b) Selectively breeding potato plants to increase the number of tubers per plant. ....

   c) Selectively breeding wheat plants to give the greatest number of grains per stalk. ....

   d) Selectively breeding sheep to increase multiple births. ....

   e) Selectively breeding beef cattle to produce the most flavoursome meat. ....

3 a) The statements below describe the various stages of the procedure used to clone Dolly the sheep. Number them **1** to **5**, to show the correct sequence of events.

   i) The embryo was inserted into the uterus of a ewe, who acted as a surrogate mother. ☐

   ii) The embryo developed into a foetus and Dolly was eventually born in the normal way. ☐

   iii) The nucleus was inserted into an egg cell that had had its own nucleus removed. ☐

   iv) The nucleus was removed from the udder cell of an adult ewe. ☐

   v) The egg was stimulated so it began to divide by mitosis to form an embryo. ☐

   b) Although animals can be cloned in this way, the procedure is still not being used in farming to increase numbers of animals. Why do you think this might be?

   ....

   ....

   ....

   ....

Divide and Develop

1) Write **true** or **false** alongside each of these statements about gene therapy, as appropriate.

a) Gene therapy is an experimental technique. ....

b) Gene therapy cures patients of a disease. ....

c) Gene therapy provides short-term relief from the symptoms of a disease. ....

d) Gene therapy involves transplanting 'healthy' genes into an individual with a genetic disease. ....

e) Gene therapy prevents a genetic disease from being passed on to the next generation. ....

2) In general terms, explain what an ethical issue is.

....

3) Gene therapy is still an experimental procedure. The questions below all need to be answered before it can become common practice.

Alongside each question, write **scientific research** or **ethical enquiry** to show what method needs to be employed to find an answer.

a) Could gene therapy increase the risk of cancer in the patient? ....

b) What are the potential side-effects? ....

c) Is it right to manipulate genes in this way? ....

d) Is the procedure safe? ....

e) Where do we draw the line between repairing damage and making improvements? ....

4) In the UK, women have the right to an abortion up to 24 weeks into a pregnancy.

a) Give one argument in favour of having the right to abort a pregnancy.

....

....

b) Give one argument against having the right to abort a pregnancy.

....

....

Divide and Develop

1 Complete the crossword below.

Across
1. These carry genes and are found in the nuclei of cells. (11)
3. The termination of a pregnancy. (8)
4. An undifferentiated cell with the potential to develop into different types of specialised cells. (4,4)
9. The process by which cells become specialised to perform different functions. (15)
11. A permanent increase in the size of an organism. (6)
12. Sex cells. (7)

Down
2. The process by which a plant cell expands, causing growth. (10)
5. A growing cluster of cells; the first stage in the development of an unborn baby. (6)
6. This type of cell division occurs during 11 across and to replace cells. (7)
7. A type of cell that divides uncontrollably, forming a tumour. (6)
8. 1 across are made from this. (3)
10. Nutrients needed by plants for 11 across. (8)

Energy Flow

1) Write a short definition for the word 'biosphere'.

....

2) Scientists think it may be possible for humans to live on Mars if an artificial biosphere was constructed. The artificial biosphere would have to incorporate sustainable sources of food, water and oxygen.

   a) What does the word 'sustainable' mean?

   ....

   b) With reference to setting up an artificial biosphere on Mars, which of these sentences describes a sustainable course of action. Use a tick ✓ to indicate your choice.

   i) Importing large quantities of tinned food, bottled water and oxygen cylinders from Earth. ☐

   ii) Establishing and maintaining enough green plants to generate sufficient amounts of oxygen and food. ☐

   c) Referring back to your answer to part **b)**, what other essential resources would the artificial biosphere need to contain to be sustainable?

   ....
   ....

3) Complete the table to show the general similarities and differences between the structures of plant and animal cells.

Feature	Plant Cells	Animal Cells
a) Nucleus		
b) Cytoplasm	✓	
c)	✓	✓
d)	✓	✗
e) Vacuole		
f)	Those that are exposed to light	

4) a) Where does photosynthesis take place in plant cells?

....

   b) What is chlorophyll?

....

Energy Flow

1 List the three factors that affect the rate of photosynthesis.

   a) ....

   b) ....

   c) ....

2 The graphs alongside shows the rate of photosynthesis in a plant on two different days.

   a) Which graph, **X** or **Y**, represents a hot, sunny day? ....

   b) Mark **D** on the graph when dawn would occur.

   c) Mark **N** on the graph when nightfall would occur.

   d) Describe, in detail, what the graphs tell you about changes in the rate of photosynthesis throughout the day.

   ....

   ....

   ....

   ....

3 Other than food, name two things that we use plants for. For each example, specify the part of the plant usually used.

   a) ....

   b) ....

HT

4 Fill in the missing words to complete this passage about plants.

Plants need to absorb .... salts from the soil. The root .... cells absorb these salts against a .... gradient. This is an example of .... transport.

The plant has to use .... from respiration to make it happen.

Energy Flow

1 The diagram alongside shows the carbon cycle.

a) How is carbon dioxide removed from the atmosphere?

b) Outline the process by which the carbon from atmospheric carbon dioxide becomes part of a carbohydrate molecule in the body of the top carnivore in a food chain.

c) Describe the two processes by which the carbon in organisms is eventually returned to the atmosphere as carbon dioxide.

i)

ii)

d) Some carbon can be removed from the cycle for very long periods of time (from hundreds to millions of years). Suggest one possible reason for this.

e) In your own words, explain why it is important for the balance of the carbon cycle to be maintained.

f) Name one human activity that generates large volumes of carbon dioxide and is therefore starting to upset the balance of the carbon cycle.

Energy Flow

1 Stephen owns a farm on which he rears beef cattle.

   a) Explain how nitrates in the soil help Stephen's grazing cattle to grow.

   b) How can nitrogen atoms in cattle be transferred to other organisms?

   c) Stephen's farm uses organic practices. The manure (waste products) from the cattle is spread on the fields. Describe what happens to the nitrogen compounds in the manure after it has been spread on the fields.

2 When Stephen first got his farm he had one field which he used for silage (grass which is cut and stored for the cows to eat over winter). He cut the grass in this field for several years and did nothing else with the land.

   a) Explain what you would expect to happen to the growth of the grass in that field over time.

   b) Describe two things that Stephen could have done to prevent this.

   i)

   ii)

3 In what way could nitrogen be removed from the nitrogen cycle for long periods of time?

Energy Flow

1 Explain what is meant by the term 'Greenhouse Effect'.

_____

_____

2 Use the graph alongside to answer the questions below.

a) i) Describe what happened to the percentage of carbon dioxide in the atmosphere over this 100-year period.

_____

_____

_____

ii) Suggest the possible reasons for this.

_____

_____

_____

b) Methane is regarded as a greenhouse gas. How would you expect the concentration of methane in the atmosphere to have changed over the same 100-year period? Explain your answer.

_____

_____

3 a) What is deforestation?

_____

b) In terms of greenhouse gases, what are the effects of deforestation?

_____

_____

_____

Energy Flow

1 a) *Obesity is a Western disease.* This quote comes from a magazine article about teenage obesity. Explain, in as much detail as you can, what it means.

....

....

....

....

b) Obesity can increase the risk of certain diseases. Name two.

i) .... ii) ....

2 a) Food shortage and famine are a big problem in the developing world. Charities arrange emergency relief to affected areas in the form of food parcels.

Explain why this is not a suitable long-term solution to the problem.

....

....

b) Suggest one other potential solution to this problem.

....

c) Give one advantage of the solution you have suggested.

....

d) Give one disadvantage of the solution you have suggested.

....

3 What are the benefits of carrying out food production in a controlled environment?

HT 4 List two ways in which commercial fish farms ensure that they produce the highest yield of fish possible.

a) ....

b) ....

Energy Flow

1 Complete the crossword below.

Across

1. The natural cycle of this element is becoming unbalanced due to human activity, e.g. burning fossil fuels. (6)
8. This pigment gives plants their green colouring and absorbs light for photosynthesis. (11)
9. Another name for mineral salts. (4)
10. This type of bacteria converts ammonium compounds into nitrates. (10)
11. This type of bacteria releases the nitrogen from nitrogen compounds. (12)

Down

1. The reaction that takes place when fuel is burned in the presence of oxygen. (10)
2. The part of the planet and its atmosphere that can support life. (9)
3. An organelle that contains 8 across; found in plant cells. (11)
4. The collective name for gases that trap heat in the Earth's atmosphere. (10)
5. The cutting down of large numbers of trees. (13)
6. Chemicals which are used to add nutrients to soil. (11)
7. The cell wall of a plant cell is made of this. (9)

Interdependence

1 a) The following information on the populations of stoats and rabbits in a particular area was obtained over a ten year period.

Year	1996	1997	1998	1999	2000	2001	2002	2003	2004	2005
Stoats	14	8	8	10	12	16	14	6	8	12
Rabbits	320	360	450	600	580	410	300	340	450	500

b) Plot a graph of these results.

c) Explain the reason for the fluctuations in the sizes of the stoat and rabbit populations.

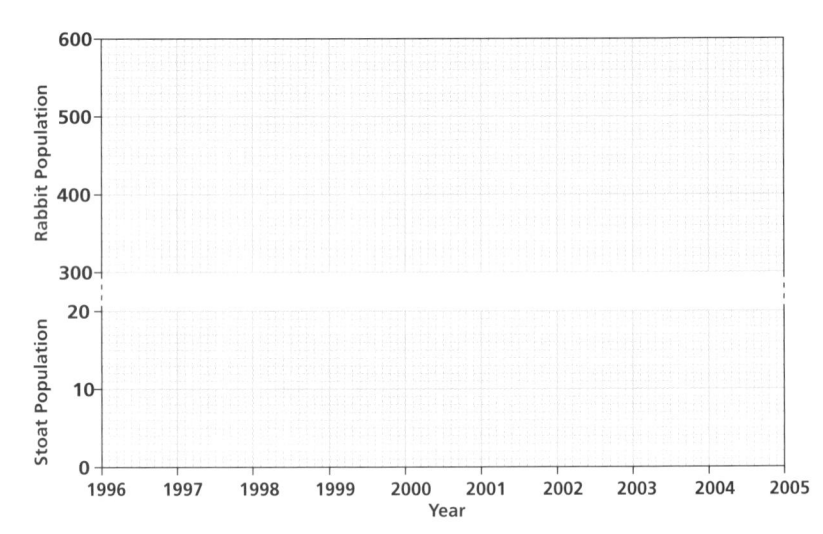

2 Unscramble the letters to find three factors that have an impact on the size of the population of a species.

a) TENPRINCENEEDED

b) NOTICEMIPOT

c) NOTAPRIDE

3 Birds' beaks are an example of adaptation. The shape and size of the beak can vary depending on what the bird eats and what else the bird uses it for. Draw a line to match each method of feeding to the correct beak.

a) A carnivorous bird that tears the flesh off animals.

b) A bird that feeds on nectar from flowers.

c) A bird that filters its food from water / mud.

d) A bird that feeds on seeds and small berries.

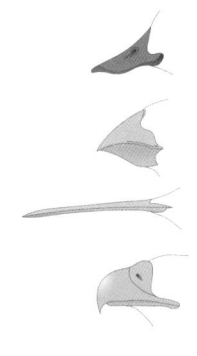

Interdependence

4 Use the words below to complete the following sentences about adaptation.

evolutionary   organism   features   survival   environment   behaviour   suited

a) Adaptations are special .... or types of ...., which make a living .... particularly well .... to its ....

b) Adaptations are part of an .... process that increases an organism's chance of ....

5 a) Design an organism (plant or animal) to live in each of the following extreme environments.

i) A hot, dry terrestrial environment (e.g. desert).

ii) The Antarctic.

i)	ii)

b) Describe the adaptations you have given each organism to help it to survive in its environment.

i) ....

ii) ....

6 List three factors that make high-altitude locations difficult places for organisms to survive.

a) ....

b) ....

c) ....

Interdependence

1) Hidden in the wordsearch are the names of six different pollutants. Once you have found them, list them below and write down the principle cause of each one.

N	I	T	A	I	L	O	T	N	O	M	V	E	S
T	O	T	A	N	K	U	E	M	H	Y	G	U	E
B	O	J	N	I	R	A	T	E	V	C	L	B	D
A	X	B	Y	T	H	U	P	O	T	P	F	H	I
W	S	I	E	R	A	Y	S	X	H	R	E	S	X
E	U	S	B	A	H	E	D	U	E	R	L	M	O
E	L	A	L	T	L	C	R	Y	C	S	A	O	I
A	F	X	A	E	D	D	D	C	A	R	B	N	D
I	R	T	Y	S	I	B	I	Q	R	T	E	P	N
H	Y	D	R	O	C	A	R	B	O	N	S	C	O
H	K	Y	X	S	H	L	R	E	L	O	T	S	B
Z	I	I	P	H	O	S	P	H	A	T	E	S	R
B	D	A	S	E	V	M	U	T	N	I	F	O	A
E	D	I	X	O	N	O	M	N	O	B	R	A	C

a) Pollutant: ....

Cause: ....

b) Pollutant: ....

Cause: ....

c) Pollutant: ....

Cause: ....

d) Pollutant: ....

Cause: ....

e) Pollutant: ....

Cause: ....

f) Pollutant: ....

Cause: ....

Interdependence

1 Giles is a farmer. He decides to sell some of his land, which is currently unused meadow land, to a property developer. The developer plans to use the site to build a small estate of family homes.

a) Describe some of the effects this will have on natural populations locally.

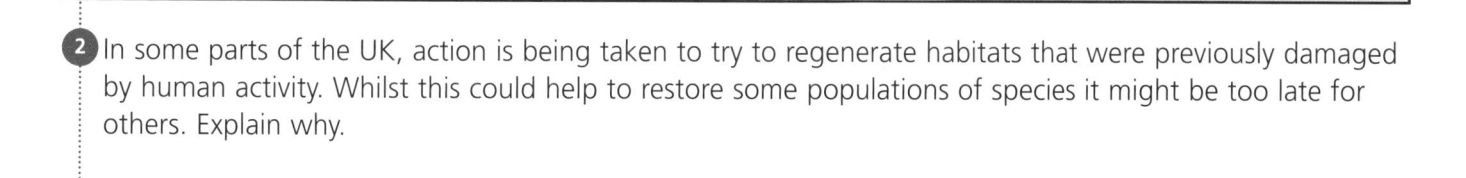

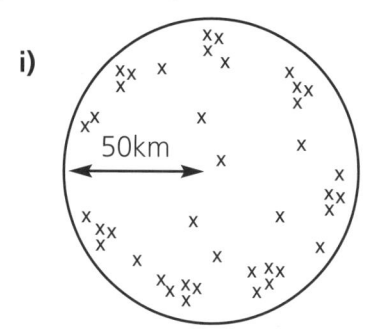

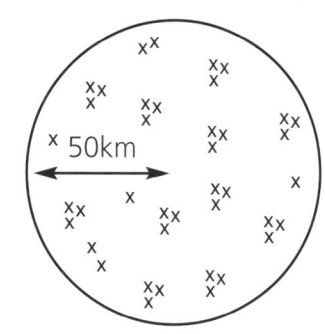

b) When all the houses have been built and sold, there will be approximately 80 more people living in the area. In terms of the environment, what problems might this cause?

2 In some parts of the UK, action is being taken to try to regenerate habitats that were previously damaged by human activity. Whilst this could help to restore some populations of species it might be too late for others. Explain why.

3 The two diagrams below show the distributions of lichens in two different regions.

i) [diagram showing lichens distributed across a 50km region]

ii) [diagram showing lichens distributed across a 50km region]

x = 100 lichens

a) In which region do you think there might be sulphur dioxide pollution? Explain your answer.

b) Draw a large spot ● on the appropriate diagram to show where the source of the pollution might be located.

Interdependence

1 An ecosystem is made up of living things and non-living things (rocks, climate, water, etc.). What other terms can be used to describe these two different factors?

a) Living things: _____ **b)** Non-living things: _____

2 List three ways in which conservation can help to maintain biodiversity.

a) _____

b) _____

c) _____

3 Choose one method of conservation. Describe, in as much detail as you can, what it involves and how it helps.

_____
_____
_____
_____

4 Below is the headline and strap line from a newspaper report.

> **IT'S GETTING HOT IN HERE!**
> But what are the consequences of
> global warming beyond warmer weather?

Explain what the term 'global warming' means.

_____
_____

5 Explain why it is better for the environment to buy a roll-on deodorant than a spray-on one in a canister that contains CFC gases.

_____
_____
_____

Interdependence

1 Complete the crossword below.

Across

3. Cutting back young trees to encourage the growth of side shoots. (9)
6. Waste substances that contaminate the environment. (10)
7. The process by which resources can be used again. (9)
8. A feature or type of behaviour which makes an organism better suited to survive in a habitat. (10)
10. The variety of organisms in an ecosystem. (12)
12. These are found in the soil and provide plants with nitrogen for growth. (8)
13. On land; on Earth. (11)

Down

1. Rivalry between organisms for resources. (11)
2. A watery environment. (7)
4. Concerned with preserving habitats and keeping ecosystems stable. (12)
5. Human organic waste. (6)
9. Used to describe environments with very harsh conditions. (7)
11. A layer of gas in the upper atmosphere, which absorbs UV radiation. (5)

Synthesis

1 Write the symbol equation for each of the reactions shown below and then balance the equations.

a) K–I + Cl–Cl ⟶ K–Cl + I–I

b) Na + Cl–Cl ⟶ Na–Cl

2 Balance the following equations:

a) $MgO + HCl \longrightarrow MgCl_2 + H_2O$

b) $Na + H_2O \longrightarrow NaOH + H_2$

c) $CuO + H_2SO_4 \longrightarrow CuSO_4 + H_2O$

d) $NH_3 + H_2SO_4 \longrightarrow (NH_4)_2SO_4$

e) $HNO_3 + CuO \longrightarrow Cu(NO_3)_2 + H_2O$

3 a) How many bonds can carbon form with other atoms?

b) How does your answer to part a) affect the type of molecules that carbon atoms can form?

c) Why are carbon compounds so important?

Synthesis

1 a) What is a hydrocarbon?

b) Explain the difference between a saturated hydrocarbon and an unsaturated hydrocarbon.

2 a) Draw the structural formulae for **i)** ethene, and **ii)** ethane.

| **i)** Ethene, C_2H_4 | **ii)** Ethane, C_2H_6 |

b) Looking at the structural formulae you have just drawn, which is an **alkane** and which is an **alkene**? Explain your answer.

3 a) Complete the following table.

Name of Compound	Methane		
Formula	CH_4		
Structural Formula			H₂C=C-C-H (with H atoms)
Description		A molecule made up of two carbon atoms, four hydrogen atoms and a double carbon-carbon bond.	

b) Which hydrocarbon in the table above is the most reactive? Explain your answer.

c) Which hydrocarbon will decolourise bromine water? Explain your answer.

Synthesis

1 a) Which process can be used to make long-chain hydrocarbons into short-chain hydrocarbons?

b) Why are short-chain hydrocarbons preferable to long-chain hydrocarbons?

c) What is meant by the term 'thermal decomposition'?

2 In the laboratory, cracking is carried out by passing long-chain hydrocarbons over a broken pot catalyst, which is being heated. What is the purpose of the broken pot catalyst?

3 An alkane chosen for cracking has the chemical formula $C_{12}H_{26}$. The equation for the reaction is:

$$C_{12}H_{26} \longrightarrow C_xH_Y + C_2H_4$$

a) Use the equation to work out the formula of C_xH_Y

b) What is the name of the hydrocarbon C_2H_4?

4 What is a monomer?

5 a) Many molecules of propene can be joined together to form poly(propene).
In the space provided, draw the structural formulae for the monomer, propene, and its polymer.

Monomer: Propene	Polymer: Poly(propene)

Synthesis

5 b) Complete the following equation to show how four propene molecules join together to form part of its polymer.

$$\underset{H\ \ H}{\overset{H\ \ CH_3}{C=C}} + \underset{H\ \ H}{\overset{H\ \ CH_3}{C=C}} + \underset{H\ \ H}{\overset{H\ \ CH_3}{C=C}} + \underset{H\ \ H}{\overset{H\ \ CH_3}{C=C}} \longrightarrow$$

6 List three useful properties that polymers can have.

a) _____

b) _____

c) _____

7 a) Draw two diagrams to show the structural difference between **i)** a thermoplastic and **ii)** a thermoset.

i) [   ]   ii) [   ]

b) Describe how the properties of a thermoplastic and thermoset differ.

_____

_____

8 Outline two ways in which the properties of plastics can be changed to produce something with more desirable properties.

a) _____

b) _____

9 As a nation we produce large amounts of plastic waste. Name the two most common methods used to dispose of plastics. For each method give one disadvantage.

a) i) Method: _____

ii) Disadvantage: _____

b) i) Method: _____

ii) Disadvantage: _____

Synthesis

1 The bar chart below shows the economic demand for the different fractions of crude oil and the relative amounts of each fraction in crude oil.

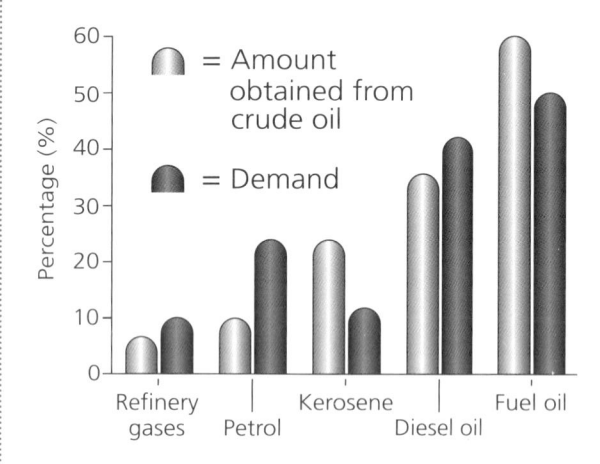

a) Which fraction is in the least demand? ....

b) For which fraction is demand two times greater than the amount available? ....

c) Name two other fractions where demand exceeds supply.

   i) ....   ii) ....

d) Explain how oil refineries match the output of different fractions to demand.

....

2 a) Explain the difference between monounsaturated and polyunsaturated fats.

....

....

b) What does the term 'viscous' mean?

....

c) Explain how monounsaturated and polyunsaturated fats can be made more viscous.

....

....

....

Synthesis

1 Choose the correct options from the words below to complete these sentences about synthesis methods.

Modelling	Target	Water	Predict	Product	Structure
Simulation	Reaction	Sustainable	Important	Yield	Waste
Reactions	Efficient	Properties	Industrial	Necessary	Programs
	Low	Drug	Hydrogen	High	

a) Computer .... can be used to .... the shape, ... and .... of the products in reactions.

b) We can predict the .... of an acid-base .... because we always get a salt and ....

c) A reaction that has a .... atom-economy is .... for .... development because it prevents ....

d) Not all .... that give a high .... are the most ....

e) Computer .... helps .... companies select the right .... compound.

2 The following sentences describe different stages in the development of new medical drugs. Number them **1** to **8** to show the correct sequence of events.

a) The structures of the new compounds are compared to existing ones. ☐

b) The new drugs are tested on cells and animals in the laboratory for toxicity. ☐

c) The most effective new drugs are tested on a large group of volunteers. ☐

d) Any compounds similar to known toxic compounds are rejected. ☐

e) Computer simulation technology is used to develop a range of new compounds. ☐

f) A final toxicology study is carried out before the drug can be licensed and manufactured. ☐

g) The remaining (target) compounds are synthesised in a laboratory. ☐

h) The new drugs are tested on a small sample group. ☐

Synthesis

1 Using the information below, calculate the relative formula mass of the listed compounds. The first one has been done for you.

Hydrogen, H	$A_r = 1$	Oxygen, O	$A_r = 16$	Sodium, Na	$A_r = 23$
Copper, Cu	$A_r = 64$	Sulphur, S	$A_r = 32$	Nitrogen, N	$A_r = 14$
Aluminium, Al	$A_r = 27$	Calcium, Ca	$A_r = 40$	Chlorine, Cl	$A_r = 35.5$
Carbon, C	$A_r = 12$				

Compound	Formula	Elements	Number of Each Element	Relative Atomic Mass, A_r	Total for Each Element	Relative Formula Mass, M_r
Water	H_2O	H O	2 1	1 16	1 x 2 = 2 16 x 1 = 16	2 + 16 = 18
Aluminium Chloride	$AlCl_3$					
Copper Oxide	CuO					
Copper Sulphate	$CuSO_4$					
Calcium Hydroxide	$Ca(OH)_2$					
Ammonia	NH_3					
Sodium Carbonate	Na_2CO_3					
Aluminium Sulphate	$AlSO_4$					

2 For each of the following compounds 'X' is an unknown element. The relative formula mass of the compound is given in brackets. Work out which element 'X' represents.

a) XO (40) _____

b) X_2O (62) _____

c) MgX_2 (94) _____

d) CX_2 (44) _____

e) X_2O_3 (188) _____

f) XCl_2 (110) _____

g) XNO_3 (63) _____

Synthesis

3 Use the following relative atomic masses to answer the questions below.

Na = 23   C = 12   O = 16   Ca = 40   S = 32   Al = 27   Cl = 35.5   N = 14

a) What is the empirical formula for the compound produced when 1.15g of sodium reacts with 0.40g of oxygen?

b) An oxide of sulphur was found to contain 40% sulphur. What is its empirical formula?

c) A compound consists of 40% calcium, 12% carbon and 48% oxygen. What is its empirical formula?

d) 2.7g of aluminium is combined with 10.65g of chlorine. What is the empirical formula of the compound produced?

e) An ammonium fertiliser is found to contain 35% nitrogen, 5% hydrogen and 60% oxygen. What is its empirical formula?

4 Calcium carbonate and hydrochloric acid react together to produce calcium chloride, carbon dioxide and water. Below is the balanced symbol equation for this reaction:

$$CaCO_{3(s)} + 2HCl_{(g)} \longrightarrow CaCl_{2(aq)} + CO_{2(g)} + H_2O_{(l)}$$

What mass of water would a tonne of calcium carbonate produce if it was fully reacted with hydrochloric acid?

Synthesis

1 a) What does the term 'atom-economy' refer to?

b) How can this help scientists?

2 The following equation shows how calcium sulphate is produced by reacting calcium carbonate with sulphuric acid. How economic is the production of calcium sulphate in this reaction?

$$H_2SO_{4(aq)} + CaCO_{3(s)} \longrightarrow CaSO_{4(aq)} + H_2O_{(l)} + CO_{2(g)}$$

(Relative masses: H = 1, O = 16, Ca = 40, C = 12, S = 32)

3 In the reaction between sulphuric acid and zinc oxide (shown below) how economic is the production of zinc sulphate?

$$H_2SO_{4(aq)} + ZnO_{(s)} \longrightarrow ZnSO_{4(aq)} + H_2O_{(l)}$$

(Relative masses: H = 1, O = 16, S = 32, Zn = 65)

4 What does the term 'yield' refer to?

5 293g of lead sulphate was obtained from the reaction of lead nitrate and sulphuric acid. What is the percentage yield of this reaction?

$$Pb(NO_3)_{2(aq)} + H_2SO_{4(aq)} \longrightarrow PbSO_{4(s)} + 2HNO_{3(aq)}$$

(Relative masses: Pb = 207, O = 16, S = 32)

Synthesis

1 Complete the crossword.

Across
3. This element is added to oils make them harder, e.g. to produce margarine. (8)
6. This describes the starting materials in all chemical reactions. (9)
9. When atoms share one or more pairs of electrons they form this type of bond. (8).
10. A thermoset is rigid and strong because its long-chain molecules are _____. (11)
13. The simplest alkene. (6)
16. Polymerisation that does not produce another substance. (8)
17. Alkenes have this effect on bromine water. (11)
18. An adverse effect of a chemical on a living organism. (8)

Down
1. Describes the process that takes place when compounds are broken down using heat. (7,13)
2. Double carbon-carbon bonds are found in this type of hydrocarbon. (11)
4. These are used to make some plastics more flexible. (12)
5. Describes a fat that contains only one double carbon-carbon bond. (15)
7. A material that can be easily softened and remoulded into new shapes. (13)
8. A method for breaking down long-chain hydrocarbons. (8)
11. The relative numbers of the different kinds of atoms or ions in a compound. (8)
12. The simplest alkane. (7)
14. A formula that gives the simplest ratio of atoms in a chemical compound. (9)
15. The name of a polymer's repeat unit. (7)

In Your Element

1 a) What is the relationship between an atom and an element?

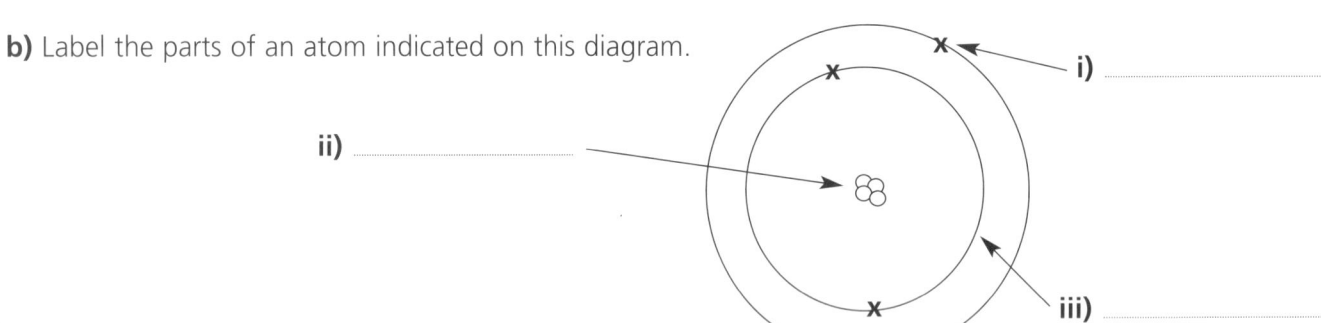

....

....

b) Label the parts of an atom indicated on this diagram.

i) ....

ii) ....

iii) ....

2 a) Complete the table about atomic particles.

Atomic Particle	Relative Mass	Relative Charge
	1	
		0
	negligible	

b) Describe the structure of the atom in terms of these particles.

....

....

3 The letters A, B, C, D, E and F represent six different elements (A, B, C, D, E and F are not the chemical symbols). Complete the table below. Use the periodic table at the back of this book to help you.

	$^{45}_{21}$A	$^{98}_{43}$B	$^{32}_{16}$C	$^{22}_{89}$D	$^{14}_{7}$E	$^{7}_{3}$F
Atomic Number						
Mass Number						
Number of Protons						
Number of Electrons						
Number of Neutrons						
Name of Element						

In Your Element

1 What is meant by the term 'isotope'?

....

....

2 Below are symbol representations of two isotopes of hydrogen.

i) $^{1}_{1}H$ ii) $^{2}_{1}H$

a) How do we know that they are isotopes of hydrogen?

....

b) How many electrons would isotope **i)** contain? ....

c) How many neutrons would isotope **ii)** contain? ....

d) What is the other isotope of hydrogen? ....

3 Uranium-235 and uranium-238 are isotopes. Are they chemically different? Explain your answer.

....

....

4 a) Naturally occurring copper contains two isotopes, copper-63 and copper-65. 69% of the atoms are copper-63 and 31% are copper-65. Use this information to calculate the relative atomic mass of copper. Remember to show all your working.

....

....

....

b) In 1000 thallium atoms there are 705 atoms of thallium-205 and 295 atoms of thallium-203. Use this information to calculate the relative atomic mass of thallium.

....

....

....

In Your Element

1 Electrons orbit the nucleus of an atom in shells.

a) Give one other name used to refer to an electron shell. _____

b) Complete the table showing the maximum number of electrons there can be in each shell.

Electron Shell	Maximum Number of Electrons in the Shell
i) 1st (innermost)	
ii) 2nd	
iii) 3rd	

2 a) Complete the following table showing the electronic properties of the first 20 elements. You can use the periodic table at the back of this book to help you.

Element	Symbol	Atomic No.	Mass No.	No. of Protons	No. of Electrons	No. of Neutrons	Electron Configuration	Group No.
Hydrogen	H	1	1	1	1	0	1	-
Helium	He	2	4	2	2	2	2	0
Lithium	Li						2,1	1
Beryllium								2
Boron				5				3
Carbon								
Nitrogen		7						
Oxygen								
Fluorine	F							
Neon								0
Sodium	Na	11						
Magnesium								
Aluminium								
Silicon		14				13	2,8,3	
Phosphorous								4
Sulphur							2,8,6	
Chlorine		17						
Argon								
Potassium	K							1
Calcium	Ca							

b) What is the link between the group number of the element and the number of electrons in its outer shell?

_____

c) Which group of elements has a full outer shell of electrons?

_____

In Your Element

3 Complete the dot and cross diagram for each of the elements below, and write its electron configuration beneath it. The first one has been done for you.

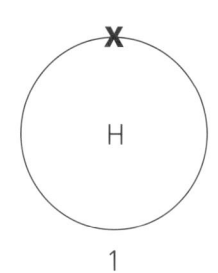

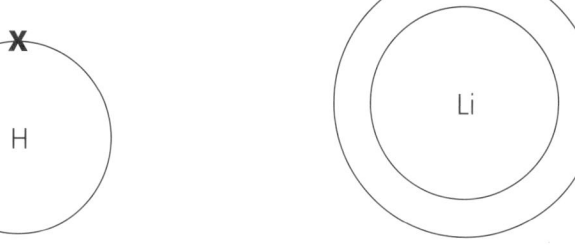

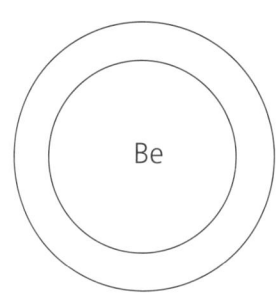

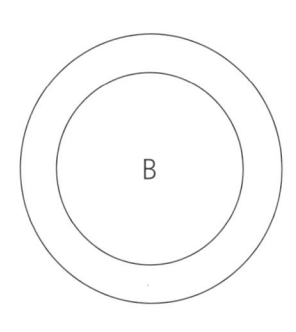

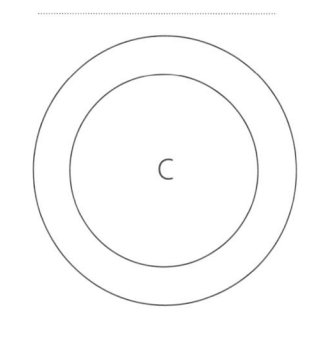

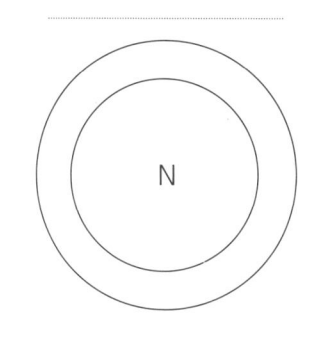

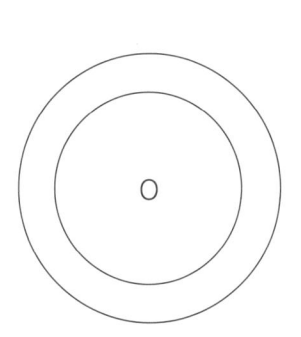

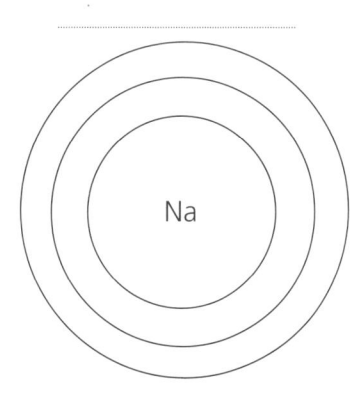

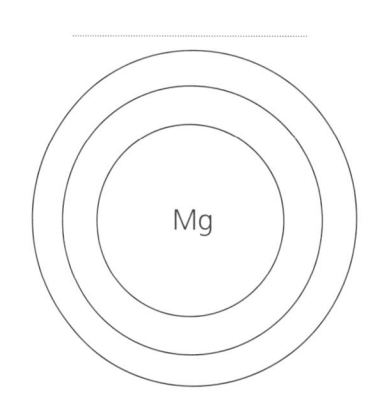

H — X (1 electron)
1

Li

Be

B

C

N

O

Na

Mg

4 a) Draw electron configuration diagrams for an atom of **Helium**, **Neon** and **Argon**.

| Helium | Neon | Argon |

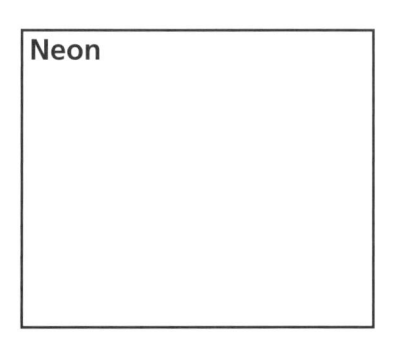

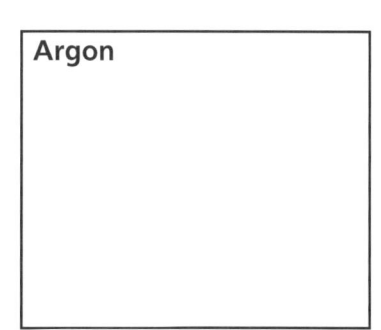

b) With reference to your diagrams, explain why the Noble gases are so unreactive.

In Your Element

1 a) What is an ion? _____

b) What type of ions do metals make? _____

c) What type of ions do non-metals make? _____

2 Choose the correct options from the words provided to complete the sentences below.

Neutral	Positively charged	Negative	Positive	Protons
Equal	Negatively charged	Fewer	Non-metal	More
	Electrons	Metal	Hydrogen	

a) Atoms are electrically _____ because they have _____ numbers of _____ (positive) and electrons (_____).

b) If electrons are taken away from a _____ atom or hydrogen then it becomes _____ because there are _____ electrons than protons.

c) If electrons are added to a _____ atom it becomes _____ because it has _____ electrons than protons.

3 Sodium and chlorine react together to produce sodium chloride. The equation for this reaction is…

$2Na + Cl_2 \longrightarrow 2NaCl$

a) Use the periodic table at the back of this book to find the atomic numbers of **i)** sodium, and **ii)** chlorine.

   i) Sodium: _____   **ii)** Chlorine: _____

b) i) In the periodic table, which group is sodium in? _____

   ii) Which group is chlorine in? _____

c) i) How many electrons does sodium have in its outer shell? _____

   ii) How many electrons does chlorine have in its outer shell? _____

In Your Element

4 a) Use a tick ✓ to indicate which of the following properties are typical of ionic compounds.

i) High boiling point ☐

ii) Low melting point ☐

iii) Conducts electricity when molten or in solution ☐

iv) Weak forces between the ions in its molecules ☐

v) Forms non-crystalline structures ☐

b) For any property that you did not tick, write out the correct equivalent property.

_____

_____

_____

5 Use the information provided to complete the table below, predicting the formula for each of the ionic compounds listed.

1+ ions
Lithium, Li^+
Sodium, Na^+
Potassium, K^+
Copper(I), Cu^+
Silver, Ag^+
Hydrogen, H^+
Ammonium, NH_4^+

2+ ions
Magnesium, Mg^{2+}
Calcium, Ca^{2+}
Copper(II), Cu^{2+}
Iron(II), Fe^{2+}
Zinc, Zn^{2+}
Lead, Pb^{2+}

3+ ions
Aluminium, Al^{3+}
Iron(III), Fe^{3+}

2- ions
Oxide, O^{2-}
Sulphide, S^{2-}
Sulphate, SO_4^{2-}
Carbonate, CO_3^{2-}

1- ions
Fluoride, F^-
Chloride, Cl^-
Bromide, Br^-
Iodide, I^-
Nitrate, NO_3^-
Hydroxide, OH^-

Compound	Positive Ion	Negative Ion	Formula
a) Zinc Bromide	Zn^{2+}	Br^-	$ZnBr_2$
b) Silver Nitrate			$AgNO_3$
c) Aluminium Chloride			
d) Sodium Nitrate			
e) Lead Sulphate			
f) Potassium Sulphate			
g) Copper(II) Sulphate			
h) Calcium Carbonate			
i) Aluminium Sulphate			

In Your Element

1 What is **a)** a cation, and **b)** an anion? Give an example for each of your answers.

a) ....

b) ....

2 a) What is a binary salt?

....

b) Give three examples of binary salts.

i) .... ii) .... iii) ....

3 Ionic compounds conduct electricity, but only when molten or dissolved in water. Explain why.

....

....

4 Choose the correct options from the words provided to complete the sentences below.

Positive electrode	Decomposition	Salt	Dissolved	Molten	Protons	Electrons
Positively charged	Electricity	Conduct	Anode	Electricity	Lose	Atoms
Negatively charged	Negative	Cations	Gain	Negative	Cathode	Free	Ions

a) Electrolysis is the .... of a compound by electricity. It uses .... to break down a .... into its elements.

b) The salts used have to be .... or .... in water before they can .... electricity, because the .... have to be .... to move around.

c) The .... ions in the salt are called .... They are attracted to the .... electrode which is called the ....

d) At the anode, the anions .... electrons to form .... or molecules.

e) The .... ions in the salt are called .... They are attracted to the .... electrode, which is called the ....

f) At the cathode, the cations .... to form atoms.

In Your Element

1 Metals are malleable.

a) What does 'malleable' mean?

b) Suggest two metal products that make use of this property.

   i) .... **ii)** ....

2 Give two practical uses for each of the following metals and explain why they are used for that purpose.

a) Iron

   i) Use 1: .... Reason: ....

   ii) Use 2: .... Reason: ....

b) Copper

   i) Use 1: .... Reason: ....

   ii) Use 2: .... Reason: ....

c) Aluminium

   i) Use 1: .... Reason: ....

   ii) Use 2: .... Reason: ....

3 a) What is the name given to a mixture of metals? ....

b) Why is this combination of metals a mixture and not a compound?

c) What benefits are there to mixing metals together?

d) Name one product which makes use of a mixture of metals instead of a pure metal and explain why.

In Your Element

1 Complete the crossword.

Across
2. This is formed when two or more elements combine. (8)
5. A metal that only contains one element. (4)
6. The type of compounds formed when a metal and a non-metal combine. (5)
8. A mixture of metals. (5)
10. Refers to the shape of an element or compound. (9)
11. Electrons have this type of charge. (8)
13. Copper is an example of this type of element. (5)
15. This number tells you the total amount of protons and neutrons in an atom. (4)
16. These subatomic particles have a positive charge. (7)

Down
1. A salt made from a cation and an anion. (6,4)
2. Another word used to describe the arrangement of electrons in an atom. (13)
3. Another word used to describe electron shells or energy levels. (6)
4. Chlorine and carbon are examples of this type of element. (3-5)
6. Atoms of the same element but with different mass numbers. (8)
7. This ion is positively charged. (6)
9. The centre or 'core' of an atom. (7)
12. The basic unit of an element. (4)
14. Atoms that lose or gain electrons to become charged. (4)

Chemical Structures

1 Choose the correct options from the words given to complete the following sentences.

| outer shell | molecules | inert | electrons | chemical |
| stable | noble | bonds | share |

Atoms join up to make _____. They do this by forming chemical _____.

A chemical bond always involves _____. A covalent bond is one where atoms

_____ one or more pairs of electrons. This means both _____ can

effectively have a full _____, which gives them a more

_____ arrangement of electrons, like that of a _____ gas.

2 a) Using the periodic table at the back of this book, complete the table below, by writing the structural formula and drawing an electron configuration diagram, for each of the elements listed.

Formula	Structural Formula	Electron Configuration
i) Cl_2	Cl-Cl	
ii) Br_2		
iii) I_2		

b) Name two things that all of the elements in the table above have in common.

i) _____

ii) _____

c) Explain why simple covalent molecules (like those in the table above) have low melting and boiling points.

Chemical Structures

1 The diagrams below show two giant covalent structures of carbon.

i)

ii)

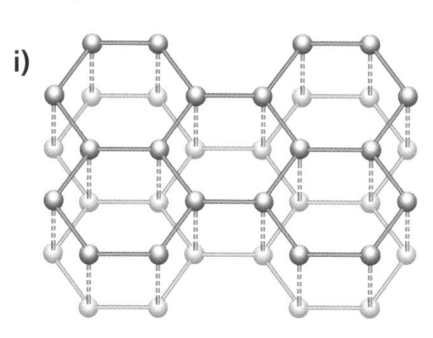

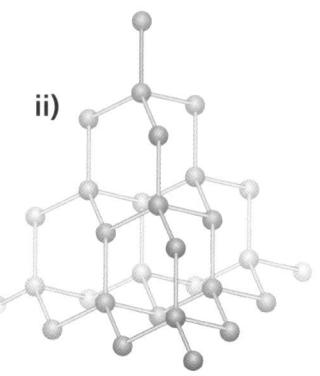

a) Which structure is **graphite** and which structure is **diamond**?

i) .... ii) ....

b) Complete the following sentences.

i) Diamond has a very high melting point because…

....

....

ii) Graphite conducts electricity because…

....

....

iii) Graphite can be used as a lubricant because…

....

....

2 a) In the box provided, draw a diagram to show how metal ions are arranged in a lattice structure.

b) Use your diagram to help explain why metals are such good conductors of electricity.

....

....

Chemical Structures

1) When a chemical substance has more than one form, each with a different chemical structure, the different forms are called allotropes. Diamond and graphite are allotropes of carbon.

Name two other important allotropes of carbon.

a) .... b) ....

2) a) What are fullerenes?

....

b) How many carbon atoms does a buckyball contain? ....

c) Write **true** or **false** alongside each of the following sentences, as appropriate.

A buckyball...

i) has a diameter of 1 nanometre. ....

ii) is stronger than diamond. ....

iii) cannot be dissolved. ....

iv) is an open carbon structure with triple carbon-carbon bonds. ....

v) can spin at very high speeds. ....

d) For each sentence that you marked as false in part c) write the correct property below.

....
....

3) a) What is CNT short for?

....

b) Why are CNTs important?

....
....

4) List two uses for **a)** carbon fullerenes, and **b)** CNTs.

a) i) .... ii) ....

b) i) .... ii) ....

Chemical Structures

1 a) What is meant by the term 'chemical-based therapy'?

....

> **b)** Give examples of two forms of chemical-based therapy and explain how they work.
>
> **i)** ....
>
> ....
>
> **ii)** ....
>
> ....

2 Look up 'homeopathy' in a dictionary. In your own words, explain what it means.

....

....

3 A homeopathic treatment for minor scalds, burns and skin irritations is urtica urens, which is an extract of common nettle. Explain, in as much detail as you can, the reason for treating burning and itching with a natural irritant.

....

....

....

....

4 Describe the main difference between the way in which conventional medicine treats illnesses and the way in which homeopathy treats illnesses.

....

....

....

5 What is the 'placebo effect'?

....

....

6 Why do scientists not believe that homeopathy is a viable method of treating illnesses?

....

....

Chemical Structures

1 Complete the crossword below.

Across
1. The non-metals found in Group 7 of the periodic table. (8)
8. An unreactive medicine that can sometimes have a psychological effect on patients, making them believe that there has been an improvement in their condition. (7)
9. Describes the electrons in a metallic structure. (4)
10. A precious gem stone made from carbon with a giant molecular structure. (7)
11. Describes the arrangement of positive ions in a metallic structure. (7)
12. The number of carbon atoms in a Buckminster fullerene. (5)
13. Refers to the forces of attraction between the molecules in a substance. (14)

Down
2. A giant structure of carbon in which each carbon atom is bonded to three other atoms by strong covalent bonds. (8)
3. Another name given to Buckminster fullerenes. (10)
4. Describes a carbon structure made from a single layer of graphite rolled into a cylinder-shape. (8)
5. A form of chemical-based therapy based on the principle of like treating like. (9)
6. The type of bond formed when atoms share electrons. (8)
7. A measure of how easily a substance allows heat or electrical energy to flow through it. (12)

How Fast? How Furious?

1 Order the following chemical reactions from **1** to **5**, with 1 being the fastest and 5 being the slowest.

a) Frying an egg ☐   b) Striking a match ☐

c) A car rusting ☐   d) Concrete setting ☐

e) Digesting food ☐

2 a) If the rate of a chemical reaction is the speed at which a reaction occurs, list three ways in which you can change the rate of reaction.

i) ....

ii) ....

iii) ....

b) Choose one of your answers to part a) and explain in detail how it helps to increase the rate of reaction.

....

....

3 a) Reactant A is a solid at room temperature and Reactant B is in aqueous solution. Place a tick ✓ alongside the conditions you would expect to produce the fastest rate of reaction.

i) A large lump of Reactant A is placed into a low concentration solution of Reactant B at room temperature. ☐

ii) Reactant A is crushed in a pestle and mortar to produce a powder, which is added to a low concentration solution of Reactant B at 40°C. ☐

iii) A large lump of Reactant A is placed in a high concentration solution of Reactant B at 50°C. ☐

iv) Reactant A is crushed in a pestle and mortar to produce a powder, which is added to a high concentration solution of Reactant B at 50°C. ☐

v) Reactant A is crushed in a pestle and mortar to produce a powder, which is added to a high concentration solution of Reactant B at room temperature. ☐

b) Explain your answer to part a).

....

....

How Fast? How Furious?

1 The word equation below shows the reaction between calcium carbonate and dilute hydrochloric acid.

Calcium carbonate + Hydrochloric acid ⟶ Calcium chloride + Water + Carbon dioxide

The rate of reaction can be studied by measuring the amount of carbon dioxide gas produced.

The graph alongside shows the results of four experiments A, B, C and D. For each experiment only the temperature of the acid was changed.

a) What must be kept constant in order to make this investigation a fair test?

....

....

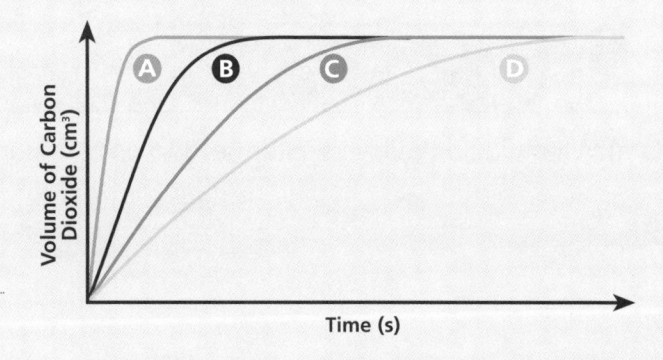

b) Which graph shows the results of the experiment with the acid at the highest temperature?

....

c) Explain your answer to part b) fully.

....

2 The graph below shows the volume of hydrogen given off during an experiment where magnesium was reacted with various concentrations of hydrochloric acid.

a) What must be kept constant in order to make this investigation a fair test?

....

....

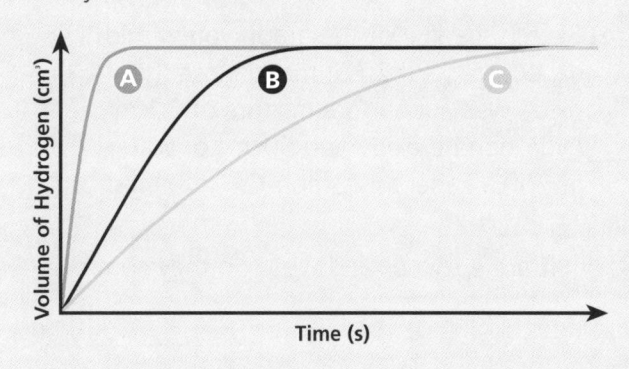

b) Which graph shows the results for the highest concentration of acid?

....

c) Explain why the total volume of gas given off was the same regardless of the concentration of the acid.

....

How Fast? How Furious?

1) The word equation below shows the decomposition of hydrogen peroxide to give water and oxygen.

Hydrogen peroxide ⟶ Water + Oxygen

Adding manganese (IV) oxide speeds up the reaction without altering the products formed.

The results below were obtained by adding 2g of manganese (IV) oxide to 100cm^3 of hydrogen peroxide at 20°C and measuring the volume of oxygen produced at 1 minute intervals.

Time (mins)	0	1	2	3	4	5
Volume of Oxygen (cm^3)	0	54	82	96	100	100

a) What would the investigator need to do to ensure this experiment was a fair test?

....

....

b) Explain how manganese (IV) oxide increases the rate of reaction.

....

....

c) Plot the results on the graph below. Label your line Graph **A**.

d) Sketch the line of the graph you would expect to get if the temperature of the hydrogen peroxide was increased to 50°C and all other conditions were kept the same. Label this Graph **B**.

e) Sketch the line of the graph you would expect to get if 2g of manganese (IV) oxide was added to a mixture of 50cm^3 hydrogen peroxide and 50cm^3 of water at 20°C. Label this Graph **C**.

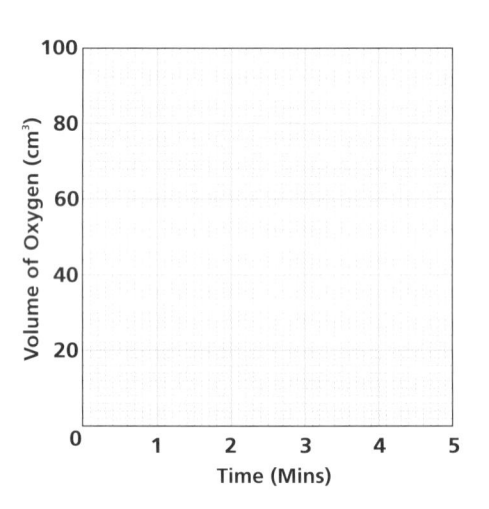

2) What are enzymes and what do they control?

....

....

....

How Fast? How Furious?

1) When ammonium chloride is dissolved in water an endothermic reaction takes place. What is an endothermic reaction?

....

2) When hydrochloric acid is reacted with sodium hydroxide in a test tube, the test tube gets hot. What is the name used to describe a reaction that gives out heat?

....

3) The equation below shows the reaction that occurs when methane burns in oxygen:

$$CH_4 + 2O_2 \longrightarrow CO_2 + 2H_2O$$

a) Which chemical bonds are broken during this reaction?

....

b) Which chemical bonds are formed during this reaction?

....

c) Is the reaction **exothermic** or **endothermic**? ....

d) How does the amount of energy needed to break the bonds in the reactants compare to the amount of energy needed to form the bonds in the products?

....

4) Carbon, in the form of charcoal, is used as a barbecue fuel. If there is enough oxygen available it will burn to produce carbon dioxide. The symbol equation for this reaction is shown below:

$$C_{(s)} + O_{2(g)} \longrightarrow CO_{2(g)}$$

a) How does the amount of energy needed to break the bonds in the oxygen (reactant) compare to the amount of energy needed to form the bonds in the carbon dioxide (product)?

....

b) Explain your answer to part a).

....

How Fast? How Furious?

1 The diagram shows an experiment where ammonium chloride is heated.

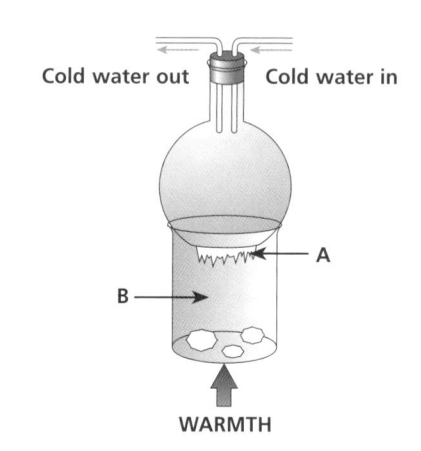

The word equation for the reaction that takes place is:

Ammonium chloride ⇌ Ammonia + Hydrogen chloride

a) What does the symbol ⇌ mean?

b) Explain why ammonium chloride is found at Point A.

c) Explain why ammonia and hydrogen chloride gas are found in the beaker at Point B.

d) Write a symbol equation for this reaction.

2 With reference to reversible chemical reactions, what is meant by the term 'equilibrium'?

3 The equation below represents a reversible reaction in equilibrium.

$$A + B \rightleftharpoons C + D$$

Changes to the conditions in which the reaction takes place can favour the forward reaction (reactants to products) or the reverse reaction (products to reactants) causing the equilibrium to shift.

For each of the changes described below, write **forward** or **reverse** to show which reaction it favours.

a) Concentration of A is increased.

b) Concentration of D is increased.

c) Concentration of D is decreased.

How Fast? How Furious?

1 a) What is ammonia, and what is ammonia used for?

....

....

b) Complete the table below, showing the advantages and disadvantages of different reaction conditions for the production of ammonia.

Reaction Condition	Advantage	Disadvantage
Low temperature		
High pressure		
Use of catalyst		

2 The Haber process is used to make ammonia.

a) Complete the diagram of the process by filling in the spaces.

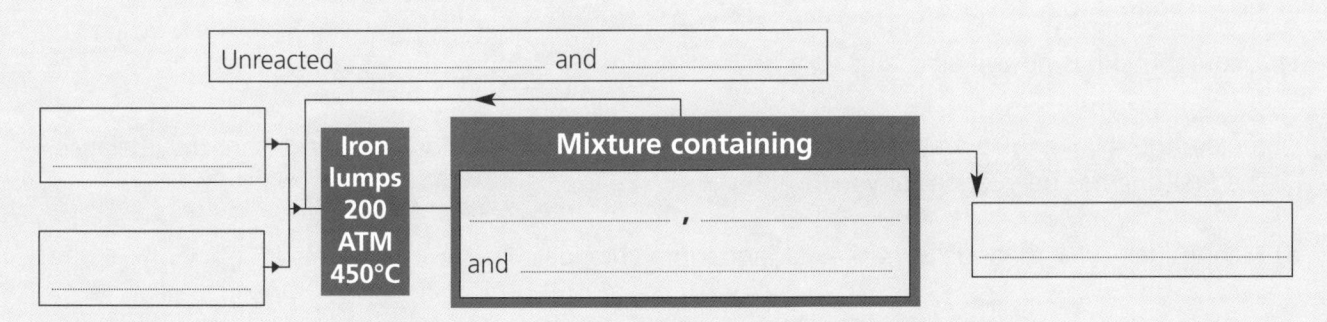

Unreacted .... and ....

Iron lumps 200 ATM 450°C

Mixture containing .... , ... and ....

b) Where are the two raw materials, nitrogen and hydrogen, obtained from?

i) Nitrogen: ....

....

ii) Hydrogen: ....

....

c) The Haber process is an example of a reversible reaction. It is carried out in a closed system so that a dynamic equilibrium is achieved.

i) What is meant by the term 'closed system'? ....

....

ii) What is meant by the term 'dynamic equilibrium'? ....

....

How Fast? How Furious?

1 a) Land which is intensively farmed requires regular applications of fertiliser. Explain why.

b) Is it more cost effective for a farmer to use artificial fertilisers or organic fertilisers? Explain your answer.

c) In terms of the environment, is it better for a farmer to use artificial fertilisers or organic fertilisers? Explain your answer.

2 Write **true** or **false** alongside each of these statements about ionic compounds, as appropriate.

a) When an atom loses electrons it forms a negatively charged ion.

b) When an atom gains electrons it forms a negatively charged ion.

c) A compound has no overall charge.

3 Complete the following equations for the formation of ionic compounds, and make sure they balance. The first one has been done for you.

a) Magnesium ion + Chloride ion ⟶ Magnesium chloride

$Mg^{2+} + 2Cl^- \longrightarrow MgCl_2$

b) Potassium ion + Nitrate ion ⟶ Potassium nitrate

$K^+ + NO_3^- \longrightarrow$

c) Magnesium ion + Sulphate ion ⟶ Magnesium sulphate

$Mg^{2+} + SO_4^{2-} \longrightarrow$

d) Ammonium ion + Sulphate ion ⟶ Ammonium sulphate

$NH_4^+ + \quad \longrightarrow$

e) Calcium ion + Chloride ion ⟶ Calcium chloride

$Ca^{2+} + Cl^- \longrightarrow$

f) Aluminium ion + Sulphate ion ⟶ Aluminium sulphate

$Al^{3+} + \quad \longrightarrow$

How Fast? How Furious?

1 Complete the crossword below.

Across
3. Describes a chemical reaction that gives off heat. (10)
4. Enzymes are this type of catalyst. (10)
6. When you do this to the temperature the reaction speeds up. (8)
9. Raising the temperature of a reaction gives 11 across more of this. (6)
10. A measure of the force exerted by a gas; caused by the impact of particles on the container wall. (8)
11. These collide together in chemical reactions. (9)
12. Any substance made from living matter. (7)
13. An interaction between two (or more) substances that results in a chemical change. (8)

Down
1. This is achieved in 7 down, when the rate of reaction in both directions is the same. (11)
2. These must take place between particles for a chemical reaction to occur. (10)
5. A biological catalyst. (6)
7. A reaction that can go both ways. (10)
8. A measure of how many particles of solute there are in a given volume of solution. (13)
11. Made in a chemical reaction. (7)

As Fast As You Can!

1) A car is travelling at a constant speed of 60mph along the motorway. How far will it travel in 2.5 hours?

2) In a local 10km running event the average speed of the winning runner was 5m/s. What was her winning time? (Give your answer to the nearest second).

3) A group of teenagers on a Duke of Edinburgh Award expedition walk at an average speed of 4kph. How far do they walk in 5.5 hours?

4) Tom's driving instructor talks about the velocity of a car. Which one of the following statements is true? Place a tick ✓ alongside the correct option.

a) Velocity is speed. ☐   **b)** Velocity is speed in a given direction. ☐

c) Velocity is the direction of the car. ☐   **d)** Velocity is speed in two directions. ☐

5) A train leaves a station and travels east in a straight line, covering a distance of 300m in 15 seconds. Work out the velocity of the train.

6) Katie walks 2km in a westerly direction in 30 minutes. She then runs back along the same route in 15 minutes. Work out…

a) Katie's walking velocity

b) Katie's running velocity

c) Katie's average speed

d) Katie's average velocity

7) Two cars are travelling with velocities of +70mph and -70mph along a motorway. Write **true** or **false** alongside the following statements, as appropriate.

a) The two cars are travelling at the same speed.

b) The two cars are travelling in the same direction.

c) The two cars are travelling at the same velocity.

d) The two cars are moving in opposite directions.

As Fast As You Can!

1 a) What is acceleration?

....

b) What is deceleration?

....

2 Write **true** or **false** alongside each of the following statements about acceleration, as appropriate.

a) Acceleration is velocity multiplied by time.　　..................

b) The units of acceleration are m/s^2.　　..................

c) Acceleration is a vector quantity.　　..................

d) Acceleration is change in velocity divided by time.　　..................

e) Acceleration relates to speed.　　..................

3 How do you calculate a change in velocity?

....

4 A lorry is stationary at a set of traffic lights. When the lights change it moves off and reaches a velocity of 15m/s after 30 seconds. Calculate the acceleration of the lorry.

....

5 A plane travelling at 240km/h lands on a runway and brakes, decreasing its velocity to 32km/h in 20 seconds. Calculate the deceleration of the plane.

....

6 A cyclist is travelling at a velocity of 6m/s and then accelerates on a downhill section at 0.8m/s^2 for 10 seconds. Work out his velocity after 10 seconds.

....

7 A car is travelling along a dual carriageway at a constant velocity. It approaches a lorry and accelerates at 50m/s^2 for 60 seconds to overtake the lorry, reaching a new velocity of 80km/h. What was the starting velocity of the car before it accelerated?

....

As Fast As You Can!

1 Alongside is a velocity–time graph for a car's journey.

   a) What was the initial acceleration of the car?

   b) What was the total distance travelled at a constant velocity?

   c) What was the total distance travelled?

   d) What was the deceleration of the car in the final part of the journey?

   e) What was the average velocity of the car for the whole journey?

2 a) What is a force?

   b) What is the unit of force? Give its full name and the correct symbol / abbreviation.

3 The diagram alongside shows a car that is moving forward.

   On the diagram draw arrows to indicate the direction of the following forces:

   a) The weight of the car.

   b) The reaction force (to the car's weight).

   c) The driving force.

   d) The resistive forces (air resistance and friction).

As Fast As You Can!

1 a) What does 'resultant force' mean?

_____

2 For each of the following questions, put a tick ✓ alongside the correct answer.

a) What is the resultant force acting on an object that is stationary?

i) <0 ☐   ii) 0 ☐   iii) >0 ☐

b) What is the resultant force acting on an object that is travelling at a constant velocity?

i) <0 ☐   ii) 0 ☐   iii) >0 ☐

c) What is the resultant force acting on an object that is accelerating (increasing in velocity)?

i) <0 ☐   ii) 0 ☐   iii) >0 ☐

3 A train is moving along a track.

→ Driving force
← Resistive force

Describe the relationship between the two forces shown when…

a) the train accelerates

_____

b) the train moves with constant speed

_____

c) the train slows down.

_____

4 The diagram shows the driving and resistive forces acting on the same car at different stages of its journey. Complete the diagrams by filling in the missing forces so that the car always has the same resultant force acting on it.

2200N ← | → 3000N   ← | → 4000N   210N ← | →

a)   b)   c)

As Fast As You Can!

1 In free-body force diagrams an arrow is used to show the direction of a force. The length of the arrow shows the size of the force. Draw a free-body force diagram for…

a) a boy sitting on the ground

b) a car being pushed

c) a hot-air balloon ascending

d) an aeroplane in flight.

2 A box of mass 10kg is on the floor. It is being pushed with a horizontal force of 10 newtons.

a) Draw a free-body force diagram showing **i)** the weight of the box, **ii)** the reaction force, **iii)** the driving force, and **iv)** the resistive force due to the friction of the floor.

b) If the box does not move, what can you say about the size of the resistive force?

c) What is the size of the reaction force?

As Fast As You Can!

1) Write down the formula that gives the relationship between force (N), mass (kg) and acceleration (m/s^2).

2) Use your formula to answer the questions below.

a) A car of mass 800kg accelerates with a driving force of 1200N. Calculate the acceleration of the car.

b) A lorry of mass 2 tonnes has a driving force of 2800N and resistive forces of 1800N. Calculate the Acceleration of the lorry.

c) A passenger train accelerates out of the station at 0.8m/s^2. If the driving force of the train is 20 000N, work out the mass of the train.

d) An aeroplane of mass 250 tonnes takes off at an acceleration of 50m/s^2. Work out the driving force of the engines.

e) A car is moving with a constant speed of 30m/s. The combined mass of the car and the driver is 1000kg.

  i) If the driving force is 3000N what is the value of the resistive force?

  ii) If the driving force is increased to 4000N calculate the acceleration of the car.

As Fast As You Can!

1) A car approaches a set of traffic lights and decelerates from a velocity of 15m/s to a standstill in 5 seconds. The combined mass of the car and the driver is 1000kg.

The spreadsheet below was set up to show the resistive force needed to produce the same deceleration if the combined mass of the car and driver increased.

1	A	B	C	D	E
2	Velocity (m/s)	Time (s)	Deceleration (m/s²)	Mass (kg)	Resistive Force (N)
3	15	5	-3	1000	-3000
4	15	5	-3	1050	
5	15	5	-3	1100	
6	15	5	-3	1150	-3450
7	15	5	-3	1200	
8	15	5	-3	1250	-3750
9	15	5	-3	1300	
10	15	5	-3	1350	
11	15	5	-3	1400	

a) Which of the following formulae would have been used in cell E3 of the spreadsheet to calculate the resistive force? Place a tick ✓ alongside the correct option.

i) =A3:D3 ☐   ii) =C3*D3 ☐   iii) =D3/B3 ☐

b) Fill in the missing values for resistive force to complete the spreadsheet above.

c) The spreadsheet below was set up to find out what would happen to the deceleration of the car if the combined mass of the car and driver increased but the resistive force remained the same.

1	A	B	C	D
2	Velocity (m/s)	Deceleration (m/s²)	Mass (kg)	Resistive Force (N)
3	15	-3.00	1000	-3000
4	15	-2.86	1050	-3000
5	15	-2.73	1100	-3000

Which of the following formulae would have been used in cell B3 to calculate the deceleration of the car? Place a tick ✓ alongside the correct option.

i) =A3*C3 ☐   ii) =C3:D3 ☐   iii) =D3/C3 ☐

As Fast As You Can!

1 The drawing shows the main forces acting on a skydiver.

Which statement correctly describes the situation shown. Place a tick ✓ alongside the correct option.

a) Force P is gravity and force Q is air resistance. ☐

b) Force P is air resistance and force Q is gravity. ☐

c) Force P is gravity and force Q is acceleration. ☐

d) Force P is acceleration and force Q is air resistance. ☐

2 The speed–time graph shows the motion of a skydiver at 10 second intervals after she steps out of the plane. The dotted line shows the point at which the parachute is opened.

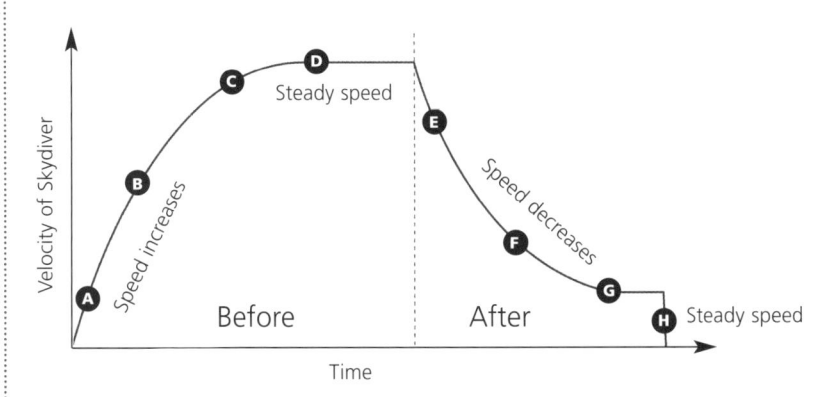

a) Explain what happens at stages A, B, C and D.

   i) A: ....

   ii) B: ....

   iii) C: ....

   iv) D: ....

b) Why is there a sudden change in velocity at stage E?

   ....

   ....

c) Explain what is happening during stages F, G and H.

   i) F: ....

   ii) G: ....

   iii) H: ....

As Fast As You Can!

1 The stopping distance of a vehicle depends on two factors. What are they?

a) _____ b) _____

2 a) Which of the following conditions might increase a car's stopping distance? Place a tick ✓ beside the correct option(s).

i) The road is dry. ☐   ii) The car is travelling uphill. ☐

iii) The car is on a motorway. ☐   iv) The road is icy. ☐

v) It is raining hard. ☐

b) Name two other factors which might affect the stopping distance of a car and explain why.

i) _____

ii) _____

3 Alongside is a speed–time graph showing a car having to make an emergency stop.

Use the graph to answer the following questions.

a) How fast was the car travelling before it braked?

b) What was the thinking distance?

c) How long did the car take to come to rest after the brakes were applied?

d) If the overall stopping distance was 56m, calculate the braking distance.

4 A car of mass 1000kg is travelling with a uniform velocity of 20m/s.

a) Calculate the car's momentum.

b) Another car of the same mass is travelling in the opposite direction at a uniform velocity of 15m/s. What is the momentum of this car?

As Fast As You Can!

1 Catherine is learning to drive. Her driving instructor points out the safety features on the car.

a) Use a tick ✓ to indicate which of the following features are **not** safety features.

i) crumple zone ☐   ii) CD player ☐

iii) seat belts ☐   iv) anti-lock braking system ☐

v) alloy wheels ☐   vi) metallic paint ☐

vii) air bag ☐

b) Pick a safety feature from the list above and explain how it works.

_____

_____

_____

c) Name two features in modern cars that are not active safety devices, but might help to reduce the risk of an accident.

i) _____

ii) _____

2 Explain what is meant by risk.

_____

3 a) Give two examples of activities where there is a risk involved but it is voluntary.

i) _____ ii) _____

b) Give two examples of activities where a risk is *imposed* on those taking part. (Hint: think about work places.)

i) _____ ii) _____

4 Why is it impossible to accurately calculate the size of a risk?

_____

_____

As Fast As You Can!

1 Complete the crossword below.

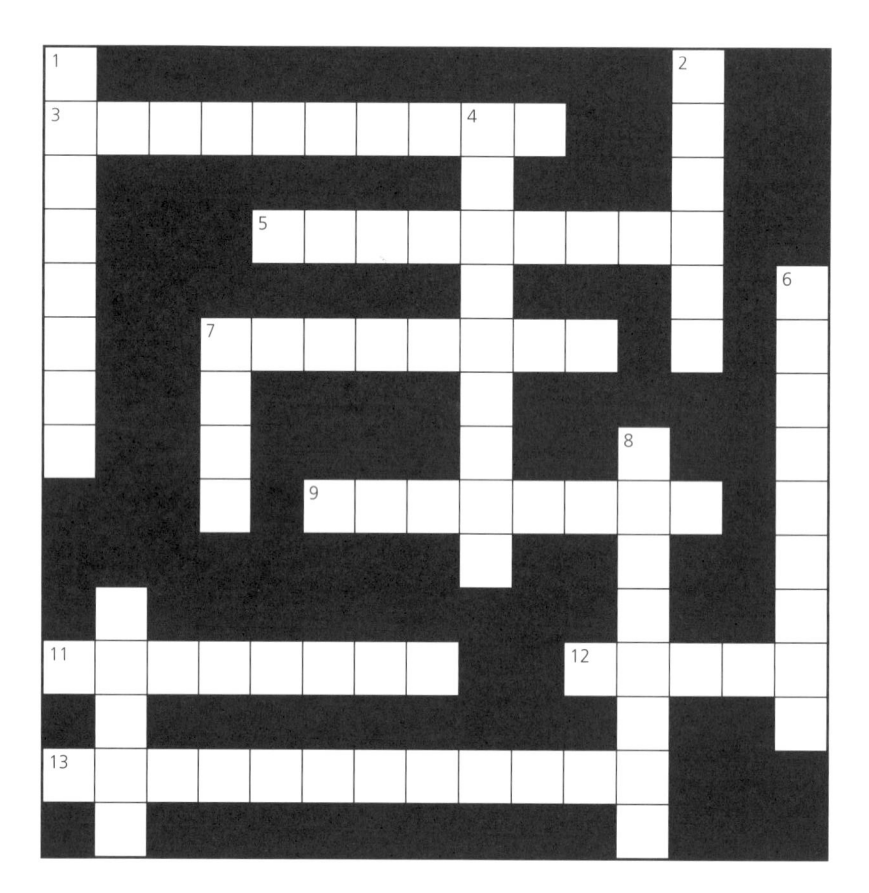

Across

3. A force that opposes motion, e.g. friction. (10)
5. The sum of all the forces acting on an object. (9)
7. A force that is equal and opposite to an action. (8)
9. The speed of an object in a particular direction. (8)
11. Describes the state of motion of an object. (8)
12. Distance travelled per unit of time. (5)
13. The rate at which an object's velocity increases. (12)

Down

1. A measure of how steep a line or slope is. (8)
2. A quantity that has both 6 down and direction. (6)
4. An impact between two or more objects. (9)
6. A measure of size. (9)
7. A perceived measure of the probability of something (often bad) happening. (4)
8. The total distance covered by a vehicle from when a driver realises he needs to apply his brakes to when the vehicle comes to a halt. (8)
10. A push or pull exerted on an object. (5)

Roller Coasters and Relativity

1 a) What is Gravitational Potential Energy (GPE)?

b) Give two examples of objects that have GPE.

   i)

   ii)

2 A skier of mass 75kg takes a chair-lift from outside his chalet. The chalet is at a height of 2300m and the top of the chair-lift is 2560m. Calculate the increase in gravitational potential energy.

3 John climbs 5m up a tree. If John's mass is 54kg work out his gravitational potential energy.

4 A football (mass 0.4kg) is kicked into the air to a height of 8m.

   a) Work out the gravitational potential energy of the ball at this height.

   b) What happens to this gravitational potential energy when the ball starts to fall back down to the ground?

5 What is Kinetic Energy (KE)?

6 Give two examples of objects that have kinetic energy.

   a)

   b)

7 A lorry of mass 2000kg is moving at a speed of 20m/s. Calculate the kinetic energy of the lorry.

Roller Coasters and Relativity

1 Write the equation used for calculating the electrical energy of an appliance.

2 In a simple electrical circuit the batteries have a combined voltage of 6V and can draw a current of 6A. If the circuit is used for 3 minutes how much electrical energy has been transferred?

3 A watch battery of 1.5 volts draws a current of 0.01A. If the battery powers the watch for 6 months (180 days) how much electrical energy has been transferred?

4 How much electrical energy does a car battery deliver in 10 seconds, if the voltage is 12 volts and it draws a current of 100A?

5 In the circuit below the lamp is switched on for 5 minutes and the reading on the ammeter is 3A.

Calculate the energy transformed.

6 Which of the following statements best describes the Principle of the Conservation of Energy? Use a tick ✓ to indicate the correct option.

a) Energy is constantly being lost, so new energy needs to be generated. ☐

b) New energy is constantly being formed, so the total amount of energy grows exponentially. ☐

c) Energy cannot be made or lost, only changed from one form into another. ☐

7 Draw a line to match each example to the correct description of how energy is transformed.

a) Using an iron	Potential energy to kinetic energy to potential energy
b) Speaking into a mobile phone	Kinetic energy to heat energy
c) A child on a park swing	Sound energy to electrical energy
d) A car coming to a stop at traffic lights	Electrical energy to heat energy

Roller Coasters and Relativity

1 Write the formula for calculating work done.

2 a) What is meant by 'power'?

b) What are the units of power?

3 Sally lifts a parcel of mass 5kg from the ground through a distance of 1.8m.

a) How much work does Sally do?

b) How much energy does Sally transfer?

c) Explain your answer to part b).

4 A cyclist moves along a level road against a resistive force of 150N. If the cyclist travels 1.5km, calculate the work done by the cyclist.

5 a) In a hydro-electric plant, 10 000kg of water are pumped back up to the upper reservoir through a distance of 120m. Calculate the work done by the pumps.

b) The process in part a) takes 3 minutes and 20 seconds. Calculate the power output of the pumps.

6 A crane on a building site lifts a load of 5000kg through a distance of 30m in 20 seconds. Calculate the power output of the crane.

Roller Coasters and Relativity

1 Give three examples of objects that travel in circular, or near circular, paths.

a) ....

b) ....

c) ....

2 For the following questions, use a tick ✓ to indicate the correct answer(s) from the options provided.

a) When an object moves in a circle it is constantly accelerating towards the centre of the circle. What does this acceleration change?

i) The speed of the object ☐   ii) The direction of motion of the object ☐

iii) The velocity of the object ☐   iv) The force of the object ☐

b) The resultant force that acts on an object to keep it moving in a circular path is called…

i) a centrifugal force ☐   ii) a reaction force ☐

iii) a centripetal force ☐   iv) a driving force ☐

c) The inward force involved in circular motion will be greater if…

i) the mass of the object increases ☐   ii) the radius of the circle increases ☐

iii) the speed of the object increases ☐   iv) the radius of the circle decreases ☐

v) the velocity of the object decreases ☐

3 John is rotating a small ball on the end of a piece of string above his head.

At point X the string suddenly breaks. Describe the motion of the ball immediately after the string breaks, and draw an arrow on the diagram to illustrate your answer.

....

Roller Coasters and Relativity

1 Most roller coaster rides begin with the cars being winched to the highest part of the ride by a powered lift.

a) What type of energy builds up during this process?

....

b) In terms of energy, describe what happens after the cars reach the highest point and begin the first descent.

....

....

c) What forces cause the cars to accelerate?

....

d) Describe how the initial height gained by the roller coaster affects the rest of the ride.

....

....

....

2 Alongside is a basic diagram of a roller coaster.

In terms of energy describe what is happening at each of the points marked on the diagram, and the impact it has on the motion of the ride.

a) ....

....

b) ....

....

c) ....

....

d) ....

....

Roller Coasters and Relativity

1 For the following questions, use a tick ✓ to indicate the correct answer(s).

a) Which of these statements best summarises the principle idea behind relativity theory?

  i) Time and space are independent concepts. ☐   **ii)** Time and space are the same concept. ☐

  iii) Time and space are relative concepts. ☐

b) Which of the following ideas formed a basis for Albert Einstein's Special Relativity Theory?

  i) Light has a constant speed. ☐

  ii) The speed of light changes depending on how fast the source is moving. ☐

  iii) All movement is relative. ☐

  iv) The speed of light from a constantly moving source is always the same. ☐

  v) Movement is discrete. ☐

c) Which of the following ideas formed a basis for Albert Einstein's General Theory of Relativity?

  i) Gravitational force is greater than inertial force. ☐

  ii) A strong gravitational field can slow things down. ☐

  iii) Gravitational force is equal to inertial force. ☐

  iv) Gravity has no effect on movement. ☐

  v) A gravitational field can bend light. ☐

d) What method did Einstein use initially to demonstrate his ideas?

  i) Thought experiments. ☐   **ii)** Practical demonstrations. ☐

  iii) Scale models. ☐

e) Which of these observations supported Einstein's General Theory of Relativity?

  i) The precession (wobble) of Mercury's axis as it orbits around the sun. ☐

  ii) Lightning striking a key suspended from a kite. ☐

  iii) The distortion (bending) of light. ☐

  iv) Red-shift in light. ☐

  v) An apple falling from a tree. ☐

Roller Coasters and Relativity

1 Complete the crossword below.

Across

3. Refers to the fact that no energy is lost or gained; it can only be changed. (12)
8. The rate at which energy is transferred. (5)
9. Something that does not change. (8)
10. Used to measure potential difference. (5)
11. Stored energy that gives a body the ability to do work. (9)

Down

1. An increase in velocity. (12)
2. The constant inward force that acts on an object moving in a circular path. (11)
4. The flow of an electrical charge. (7)
5. A theory proposed by Albert Einstein. (10)
6. The energy possessed by a moving object. (7)
7. The type of energy most often used in the home to power appliances. (10)

Putting Radiation to Use

1 The diagram below shows a simple model of a lithium (Li) atom. Lithium has an atomic number of 3 and a mass number of 7.

Name the particles X, Y and Z.

a) X = ... **b)** Y = ... **c)** Z = ...

2 The atomic number of cobalt is 27. Cobalt has two isotopes: cobalt-60 and cobalt-59.

a) What is an isotope?

....

....

b) Fill in the missing information about the two isotopes of cobalt to complete the table below.

	Cobalt-60	Cobalt-59
i) Number of protons		
ii) Number of neutrons		
iii) Number of electrons		

3 What do we mean if we say a substance is radioactive?

....

4 Use lines to link the different types of radiation to the relevant description(s). A description can apply to more than one type of radiation.

- **a)** Alpha
- **b)** Beta
- **c)** Gamma

- Emitted from a nucleus
- Very high frequency radiation.
- Consists of two protons and two neutrons.
- Very short wavelength radiation.
- Fast moving electron.
- Has a negative charge.
- A helium nucleus.

5 What do we mean when we talk about the 'activity' of a radioactive isotope?

....

Putting Radiation to Use

1 What is meant by the term 'half-life'?

_____

2 The half-life of radioactive carbon is 5730 years. How long will it take for a sample of radioactive carbon to become $\frac{1}{4}$ as active as it is now? Use a tick ✓ to indicate your answer.

a) 1432.5 years ☐

b) 2865 years ☐

c) 5730 years ☐

d) 11 460 years ☐

3 Different radioactive materials have very different half-lives. The graph below shows the decay of a radioactive substance.

What is the half-life of this material?

_____

4 Knowledge about the half-lives of radioactive elements can be used to date certain materials by measuring the amount of radiation they emit. Name two materials that can be dated using this technique.

a) _____ b) _____

5 A Roman dagger was found and dated at 1900 years old. Why must we assume that the dagger is not exactly 1900 years old? Use a tick ✓ to indicate your answer.

a) The dagger is too shiny to be that old. ☐

b) Measuring the activity of the radioactive material is a modern technique. ☐

c) Measuring the activity of the radioactive material is not 100% accurate. ☐

Putting Radiation to Use

1) A radioisotope emits beta particles. It has a half-life of 1.5 days. The starting mass of active isotope is 200g. What mass of active isotope will remain after…

a) 1.5 days? ....   b) 3 days? ....

c) 6 days? ....   d) 12 days? ....

2) Americium-241 is used in smoke detectors. It has a half-life of 460 years. How long will it take a sample of americium-241 to decrease to $\frac{1}{8}$ of its original number of radioactive atoms?

3) The explosion at the Chernobyl Nuclear Reactor released a large cloud of radioactive gas into the atmosphere which spread over Europe. The gas contained caesium-137 (with a half-life of 30 years) and iodine-131. The following table shows measurements of the count rate from a small amount of iodine-131:

Time (Days)	0	4	8	12
Count Rate (Counts/s)	320	250	160	85

a) From the table work out the half-life of iodine-131.

b) Four months after the explosion scientists were no longer concerned about the health risks from the iodine but were still worried about the effects from the caesium-137. Do you think they were right to be concerned? Explain your answer.

4) Of the three types of radiation, which one would be absorbed by a few millimetres of thin metal?

5) a) What is meant when an atom is referred to as an 'ion'?

b) When radiation is described as having ionising power, what does this mean?

c) Number the three types of radiation on order of their ionising power, where **1** is the strongest ionising power and **3** is the weakest.

Alpha ☐   Beta ☐   Gamma ☐

Putting Radiation to Use

1) Why is ionising radiation dangerous to humans?

2) The damaging effects of radiation depend on whether the radiation source is outside or inside the body.

   a) Which type(s) of ionising radiation is not harmful when the source is outside the body, and why?

   b) Which type(s) of ionising radiation is not harmful when the source is inside the body, and why?

3) Radiotherapy has been shown to slow down the spread of cancerous cells. Describe one way in which ionising radiation is used in radiotherapy treatment.

4) Radiation can be used to sterilise medical instruments.

   a) What type of radiation would be best suited for this job?

   b) How does the radiation make the instruments sterile?

   c) What is the advantage of this method over more conventional techniques?

5) What property of X-rays means they can be used to produce X-ray photographs of bones?

Putting Radiation to Use

6) Radiation can be used to preserve food. Explain how it works.

....

....

7) The diagram below shows a simple smoke detector.

a) Explain what happens when the alpha particles pass between the electrodes.

....

....

b) Explain what happens if smoke enters the space between the two electrodes.

....

....

8) The diagram shows a method of controlling the thickness of steel. A radioactive source which emits gamma rays is placed on one side of the steel and a detector is placed on the other.

a) How will the amount of radiation detected change as the steel gets thicker?

....

b) How will the machine respond to this change?

....

c) Explain in detail why a radioisotope which emits alpha or beta particles could not be used for this job.

....

How Fast? How Furious?

1) Uranium is found naturally in granite rock. Radon gas is a colourless, odourless gas which is produced during the radioactive decay of uranium. Explain why this may be a potential hazard.

....

....

....

2) The following table shows a breakdown of the amount of radiation produced by various sources.

Source of Radiation	Dose (Arbitrary Units)
Radon	0.50
Medical	0.12
Nuclear Industry	0.01
Cosmic Rays	0.10
Gamma Rays	0.15
Food	0.12
TOTAL	**1.00**

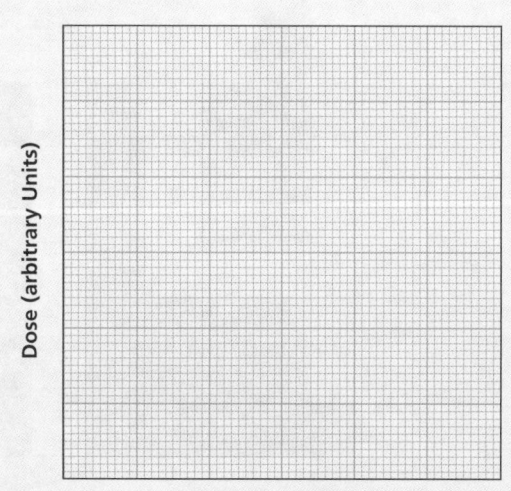

a) Draw a bar chart to display this data.

b) What percentage of background radiation is from man-made sources?

....

3) The Earth has two features that protect it, and us, from harmful radiation.

a) What are the names of these two features?

i) ....

ii) ....

b) Choose one of these features and explain, in as much detail as you can, how it protects the Earth.

....

....

....

Putting Radiation to Use

1 Complete the crossword below.

Across

1. A colourless radioactive gas. (5)
3. Rays of high-frequency electromagnetic radiation. (5)
7. This number is equal to the number of protons in one atom of a particular element. (6)
11. The use of ionising radiation in the treatment of cancer. (12)
14. This type of radioactive particle is a fast-moving electron. (4)
15. The time taken for 50% of the undecayed nuclei in a radioactive substance to decay. (4-4)

Down

2. Used to describe the new generation of nuclei produced by the radioactive decay of a parent nucleus. (8)
4. The average number of disintegrations that occur per second in a radioactive substance. (8)
5. This number is equal to the sum of all the protons and neutrons in one atom of a particular element. (4)
6. This occurs when radiation knocks an electron out of the shell of an atom. (10)
8. Spontaneous changes in the structure of cells that can be caused by radiation. (9)
9. The state of a radioactive nucleus. (8)
10. The unit of 4 down. (9)
12. This type of radioactive particle is made up of two protons and two neutrons. (5)
13. Atoms of the same element, which have different numbers of neutrons. (8)

Power of the Atom

1 Einstein's famous equation connects two fundamental properties together in one equation, as shown below:

$$E = mc^2$$

a) What do the following symbols represent?

i) E = ... ii) m = ... iii) c = ...

b) According to Einstein's equation, the small amount of energy lost during nuclear fission is translated into enormous energy gain. What happened for the first time in 1943 to verify this theory?

....

2 What happens during nuclear fission?

....
....

3 The diagram below shows part of a nuclear fission process. Write the following labels in the correct places on the diagram.

| Further neutrons | Energy | New radioactive nuclei are formed | Uranium nucleus |
| Unstable nucleus | Neutron | Fission occurs (nucleus splits) | |

4 a) What are the products of nuclear fission?

....

b) Are these products **radioactive** or **non-radioactive**? ....

c) What potential problem does this pose?

....
....

Power of the Atom

1) Once nuclear fission has started it continues by itself.

a) What is the term used to describe a self-sustaining reaction like this?

_____

b) Describe, in as much detail as you can, how the reaction continues by itself.

_____

_____

_____

c) Use a diagram to show the sequence of events you described in part b) up to a third generation.

2) Manipulating a chain reaction allows it to be used in two very distinct ways.

a) A controlled chain reaction can be used to produce heat. What is the heat then used for?

_____

_____

b) An uncontrolled chain reaction can be used to generate a massive amount of energy. What is this energy used for?

_____

3) The following sentences describe the different processes that occur in a Pressurised Water Reactor (PWR) to generate electricity. Number them **1** to **6** to show the correct sequence of events.

a) The turbines rotate to generate electricity (electrical energy). ☐

b) The cooled water is returned to be re-heated by the reactor. ☐

c) A step-up transformer is used to take the electricity to the National Grid via pylons. ☐

d) Steam from the boiler drives the turbines. ☐

e) Heat from the reactor is used to make steam. ☐

f) The steam cools to produce water. ☐

Power of the Atom

1 a) Give three advantages of using a Nuclear Power Station to generate electricity.

   i) ....

   ii) ....

   iii) ....

b) Give three disadvantages of using a Nuclear Power Station to generate electricity.

   i) ....

   ii) ....

   iii) ....

c) Name two alternative sources of natural energy that could be harnessed to produce electricity.

   i) ....   ii) ....

HT 2 Explain what happens during the nuclear fusion process.

....

....

3 Name two conditions that must be met before nuclear fusion can take place.

   a) ....   b) ....

4 Use the words supplied to label the products on the diagram and show how the Sun produces light and heat energy.

   Deuterium   Tritium   Helium   Neutron   Energy and Light

   Fusion

5 Explain the difference between nuclear fission and nuclear fusion.

....

....

Power of the Atom

1 Explain what is meant by the term 'static electricity'.

2 Paul rubs a balloon on his jumper, charging it with static electricity.

   a) Explain how the balloon gains a positive charge.

   b) What charge will Paul's jumper now have?

3 Karen was in her classroom, which has a nylon carpet. She found that walking over the carpet and touching the metal radiator gave her an electric shock. Explain why this happened.

4 Write **attraction** or **repulsion** alongside each of these combinations to show the response they will produce.

   a) negative – positive _____   **b)** positive – positive _____

   c) negative – negative _____   **d)** positive – negative _____

5 Two ebonite rods are rubbed with fur. One of these rods is suspended from a string. What will happen to the suspended rod if the other rod is moved close to it? Explain your answer.

6 A charged ebonite rod is moved close to a suspended and charged Perspex rod. What will happen to the suspended rod? Explain your answer.

Power of the Atom

1 Clouds become charged due to very small particles of ice rubbing against each other. In thunder clouds the charge is greater than normal and lightning can occur.

a) What is lightning?

b) If thunder clouds gain a negative charge, explain clearly how discharge occurs.

2 Some buildings have a lightning conductor fixed to the outside wall. This is a copper rod which rises above the highest part of the building with its lower end connected to earth. Explain, in as much detail as possible, how this protects the building from lightning.

3 Give two examples of everyday products that make use of static electricity.

a) _____ **b)** _____

4 The following statements describe how a laser printer works. However, they are mixed-up. Number them **1** to **6** to show the correct sequence of events.

a) Paper is heated to fix the final image. ☐

b) Powder is transferred from the plate to the paper. ☐

c) Charged impression of the plate attracts tiny specs of black powder. ☐

d) Charge leaks away due to light, leaving an electrostatic impression of the page. ☐

e) Image of the page to be copied is projected onto the plate. ☐

f) Copying plate is electrically charged. ☐

Power of the Atom

1) During the refuelling of planes, care has to be taken to avoid dangerous electrical discharges.

   a) Explain how a discharge could occur.

   b) Explain what action can be taken to make the process safer, and how it works.

2) a) Explain why static electricity is a real hazard at a petrol station.

   b) List three precautions that should be taken at a petrol station to avoid the discharge of static electricity.

   i)

   ii)

   iii)

3) a) Explain how computers can be damaged by static electricity.

   b) Describe two precautions that computer technicians can take to avoid damaging computers with static electricity.

   i)

   ii)

4) Explain what 'earthing' means.

Power of the Atom

1 Complete the crossword below.

Across

3. The splitting of atomic nuclei. (7)
4. The joining together of nuclei. (6)
7. Electricity produced by friction; does not move. (6)
8. Another name for heat energy. (7)
10. This allows electrons to flow from one object to another to encourage discharge. (8)
11. The joining together of nuclei at low temperatures. (4,6)
12. This results in materials of the same charge pushing away from each other. (9)

Down

1. A material that allows electrical energy to flow through it easily. (9)
2. A material that does not allow electricity or heat to flow through it easily. (9)
5. This results in two materials of different charges being drawn together. (10)
6. This type of reaction is self-sustaining. (5)
9. The device in which 3 across takes place inside nuclear power stations. (7)

Notes